Modern Native Feasts

MODERN

Healthy, Innovative, Sustainable Cuisine

NATIVE

ANDREW GEORGE JR.

FEASTS

ARSENAL PULP PRESS  VANCOUVER

ARSENAL PULP PRESS
Suite 202 – 211 East Georgia St.
Vancouver, BC V6A 1Z6
Canada
arsenalpulp.com

The publisher gratefully acknowledges the support of the Government of Canada (through the Canada Book Fund) and the Government of British Columbia (through the Book Publishing Tax Credit Program) for its publishing activities.

The author and publisher assert that the information contained in this book is true and complete to the best of their knowledge. All recommendations are made without a guarantee on the part of the author and publisher. The author and publisher disclaim any liability in connection with the use of this information. For more information, contact the publisher.

Note for our UK readers: measurements for non-liquids are for volume, not weight.

Design by Gerilee McBride
Cover and interior photographs and food styling by
    Tracey Kusiewicz, Foodie Photography
Author photograph, page 9: Rob Gilbert
Editing by Susan Safyan

Printed and bound in Canada

Library and Archives Canada Cataloguing in Publication

George, Andrew, author
    Modern native feasts : healthy, innovative, sustainable cuisine / Andrew George Jr.

Includes index.
Issued in print and electronic formats.
ISBN 978-1-55152-507-5 (pbk.).—ISBN 978-1-55152-508-2 (epub)

    1. Indian cooking. 2. Indians of North America—Food—Canada. I. Title.

TX715.6.G4586 2013   641.59'297071   C2013-903243-6
                                            C2013-903244-4

I would like to
dedicate this book to my spouse,
Cecilia, and our wonderful children,
Mckayla and Andrew, for their support,
patience, and numerous sacrifices throughout my
culinary journey. I would also like to welcome our
granddaughter, Sophia, to the family.

To all my culinary students, past, present, and future,
I hope this book inspires you to take your career in
the world of Aboriginal cuisine to the next level,
and to be proud of who we are and where
we come from.

CONTENTS

INTRODUCTION

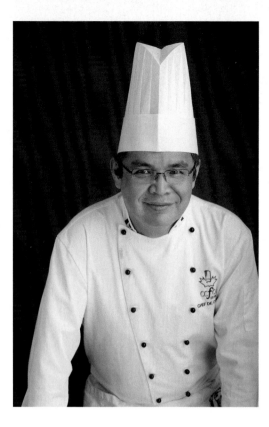

I grew up in Telkwa, British Columbia, the third eldest of six kids. Our home didn't have indoor plumbing or running water. For food, my family and I had to take advantage of what was available to us seasonally, in the wild. In the spring and summer, we would harvest trout and salmon; in the fall, we would hunt moose, rabbit, and deer; in the winter we would go ice fishing. Aboriginal people have a strong tie to the land and to their traditions, and it has always been my goal to fuse these traditional values with modern and innovative cooking techniques. With that in mind, at the age of 18, I decided to become a chef.

In 1983, I was accepted into the Vancouver Vocational Institute (now Vancouver Community College) for culinary training, and I graduated in 1985. I continued my education by taking apprenticeship programs through the British Columbia Institute of Technology. While still apprenticing, I became the head grill cook for the First Nations Restaurant at the Folk Life Pavilion at Expo '86 in Vancouver. I continued my apprenticeship afterward at

The SuperChefs of the Universe program was originally created by Vancouver chef, clown, and dentist Greg Chang to help fight childhood diabetes and obesity by teaching kids the joys of cooking. In 2012, I established the first Indigenous SuperChefs Camp with them. We taught the kids not only how to cook, but also how to create meals that were traditional and healthy. On National Aboriginal Day (June 21), the kids cooked for more than a hundred Kwakwaka'wakw District Council community members, and they've since participated in several local food festivals. SuperChefs will continue to host a camp annually to provide kids with the great opportunity to learn how to cook with some of the best Aboriginal chefs in British Columbia.

Avenue Grill in Vancouver before completing my training at Isadora's Restaurant on Granville Island (in Vancouver) in 1989.

In the early '90s, I decided to open my own business, the Toody Ni Grill and Catering Company, which specialized in Northwest-style Native cuisine. In 1992, I was chosen as a representative for the Aboriginal peoples of Western Canada, along with four other Native chefs from across Canada, to participate in the World Culinary Olympics in Frankfurt, Germany. This event was attended by 13,000 people from more than fifty-four different countries, and we were the first Aboriginal team from anywhere in the world to compete at that level.

After the 1992 Culinary Olympics, I was part of a group that assisted in the development of program curriculums and recipes designed to encourage Aboriginals to join the cooking trade, which is how I ultimately began my teaching career. I moved to Montreal, where I co-taught a course at the Institut de tourisme et d'hôtellerie du Québec. While there I was given the opportunity to travel all over Canada speaking with Native elders on how they traditionally harvested, gathered, and preserved their food. I brought this wealth of information back to my class in Montreal, where I used it to develop new, modern versions of the recipes I had heard about.

In 1997, my first cookbook, *Feast!: Canadian Native Cuisine for All Seasons* was released. *Feast!* featured basic recipes that introduced the reader to traditional Aboriginal cuisine and showed them simple and rustic ways of preserving and preparing Indigenous foods based on the four seasons: spring, summer, fall, and winter, and the four elements: Air, Water, Land (animals), and Earth (fruits, grains, vegetables). It also included stories of how we hunted and gathered traditional foods. The recipes from *Feast!* have been used as guides for menus in major hotels around the world, from Berlin and Frankfurt to Montreal, Toronto, Calgary, and Vancouver.

I moved back to the Vancouver area in 2006 and began teaching a pre-apprenticeship culinary arts program. I also began to develop my skills and repertoire at special events by speaking at elementary and high schools and in post-secondary culinary classes, sharing my love of Aboriginal cuisine with the students I met. One of the biggest events my students and I participated in was the 2010 Canadian Culinary Federation's National Chefs Conference, where we prepared an Aboriginal-themed menu for chefs from across Canada.

Feast! was re-released by Arsenal Pulp Press prior to the 2010 Winter Olympics in Vancouver with some modifications, including a new cover, new pictures, and new recipes. It was also given a new name, A Feast for All Seasons: Traditional Native Peoples' Cuisine. The re-release of my cookbook and the 2010 Winter Olympics marked an important turning point for me; I was head chef for the Four Host First Nations Pavilion at the Winter Olympics as well as for a number of different official events—from the one in 2003 announcing Vancouver as host of the 2010 Winter Olympics to the one held the night before the Games opened. This not only gave me the opportunity to make the Aboriginal component of the official Olympics menus stand out, but also gave attendees the chance to try many of these recipes for the first time.

In 2012, I took part in designing a pilot version of the Professional Cook Level 1 training program at Tsleil-Waututh for Aboriginal people interested in becoming Red Seal chefs (the Canadian interprovincial standard of excellence in the trades). More recently, I joined SuperChefs of the Universe (see sidebar), a program designed to promote healthy eating and lifestyle habits in children and combat childhood diabetes. This allows me be to a part of the movement to introduce Aboriginal children to the importance of eating local, fresh ingredients while maintaining tradition.

I have had the good fortune of sharing Aboriginal food and culture with those who live in the remote corners of Canada and beyond; in September 2012, I even had the honor of touring the United States with a group of chefs from around the world.

But I felt I had more to share about Aboriginal cuisine. Since the release of A Feast for All Seasons, I've been collecting the recipes I'd used at events, banquets, dinners, and catering events throughout North America and Europe. Knowing that, since 1997, the landscape of Aboriginal cuisine has changed, I wanted to give people the opportunity to understand and participate in that change.

Modern Native Feasts is the product of this change and a reflection of my own desire to return to the idea of fusing the traditional with the modern. These recipes combine the use of fresh, local, and seasonal products with contemporary ways of approaching traditional forms of cooking, such as brining, smoking, and curing. Most of the ingredients are readily available and affordable, and I've suggested alternatives where they might be useful as well as healthier options to traditional ways of preparing some of these dishes.

Modern Native Feasts is inspired by the wonderful chefs and people that I have met on my journey throughout North America and Europe who continually strive to promote and develop Aboriginal cuisine and culture. I am indebted to my family and the Wet'suwet'en people who have assisted my development in the culinary arts. I hope this collection of recipes inspires you as much as it has me, and that you will share these recipes with your family and friends.

Messi,
Chef Andrew George, Jr, Skit'den (traditional hereditary wing chief name of the Wet'suwet'en people)

STOCKS, SAUCES, SPREADS & DIPS

FISH STOCK

Fresh fish stock makes all the difference to the flavor of chowders, soups, and sauces—and it's so easy. Note: *Always prepare stocks with cold water.*

◀ Makes 3 cups (1.5 L) ▶

3 lb (1.5 kg) halibut bones

1 leek (white part only), chopped

1 large onion, chopped

1 celery stalk, chopped

6 cups (1.5 L) cold water

½ cup (125 mL) white wine

2 lemons, cut in half lengthwise

1 bouquet garni (see below)

In a large stock pot, combine all ingredients. Bring stock to a boil. Reduce heat to low and allow to simmer and reduce for 45 minutes. With a slotted spoon, periodically remove scum from surface. Strain through a fine mesh and use as a base for soups, stews, and sauces.

BOUQUET GARNI

A bouquet garni is often used to add flavor to soups, stocks, and stews. Typically, it contains a number of different herbs and sometimes spices, and can be tied together inside a small square of cheesecloth using string or butcher twine.

1 bay leaf
1 tsp crushed peppercorns
2–3 sprigs fresh parsley
2–3 sprigs fresh thyme

CHICKEN STOCK

This stock makes a great base for soups, sauces, and stews. Its neutral flavor will complement poultry, meat, and even fish. **Note:** *Always prepare stocks with cold water.*

Makes 3 cups (1.5 L)

3 lb (1.5 kg) chicken bones

1 large carrot, chopped

1 large onion, chopped

1 celery stalk, chopped

6 cups (1.5 L) cold water

1 bouquet garni (p. 14)

In a large stock pot on high heat, bring all ingredients to a boil. Reduce heat to low and let simmer and reduce for 2 hours. With a slotted spoon, periodically remove scum from surface. Strain and use as a base for soups, stews, or sauces.

BROWN STOCK

Professional chefs know that making stock from scratch, though a time-consuming process, is well worth the effort. Use this recipe as a base for extraordinary gravies, demi-glace (p. 20) or sauces such as Espagnole sauce (p. 19).

Makes 4 cups (1 L)

3 lb (1.5 kg) beef bones

¾ lb (375 g) veal leg bones

1 large carrot, chopped

1 large onion, chopped

1 celery stalk, chopped

1 tbsp tomato paste

8 cups (2 L) cold water

1 bouquet garni (p. 14)

Preheat oven to 350°F (180°C).

Spread bones evenly in a deep roasting pan and roast until they start to caramelize, about 45 minutes. Add carrots, onions, and celery and roast for an additional 20 minutes. Spread tomato paste evenly over roasted bones and vegetables and roast for another 20 minutes, until tomato paste is a deep brown color. Transfer roasted mixture to a large stock pot and add water and bouquet garni. On high heat, bring stock to a boil. With a slotted spoon, remove scum from surface. Reduce heat to low and let simmer, uncovered, for 4 hours.

Strain out bones and vegetables. Transfer stock to a smaller stock pot. On medium heat, reduce by half (from 8 to 4 cups) then pour into a shallow pan. Cool and store in refrigerator in a covered container for up to 7 days. If prepared properly, stock should gel.

GAME STOCK

For me, this recipe brings back memories of our elders, who always had a pot of moose-bone soup simmering on the woodstove for anyone who might stop by. It makes a great base for Elk Stew (p. 93) and other stews and soups.

Makes 4 cups (1 L)

3 lb (1.5 kg) venison bones

8 cups (2 L) cold water

1 large carrot, chopped

1 large onion, chopped

1 celery stalk, chopped

1 bouquet garni (p. 14)

Preheat oven to 350°F (180°C).
In a large stock pot on high heat, add all ingredients, in order listed, and bring to a boil. With a slotted spoon, remove scum from surface. Reduce heat to low and let simmer for 4 hours.

Strain out bones and vegetables and transfer stock to a smaller pot. Continue to simmer until reduced by half, to 4 cups (1 L). Pour stock into shallow pan and cool. Store in refrigerator in a container with a tight-fitting lid until used. If prepared properly, stock should gel.

ESPAGNOLE SAUCE

This is considered one of the five "mother" sauces of classical French cooking.
It's used as a base for demi-glace (p. 20) and other sauces.

Makes about 3 cups (750 mL)

½ cup (125 mL) butter

1 medium carrot, coarsely chopped

1 small onion, coarsely chopped

1 celery stalk, coarsely chopped, leaves included

¼ cup (60 mL) all-purpose flour

4 cups (1 L) hot brown stock (p. 16)

¼ cup (60 mL) tomato purée

2 garlic cloves, finely chopped

⅛ tsp ground black pepper

1 small bouquet garni (p. 14)

In a large saucepan on medium heat, melt butter. Sauté carrots, onions, and celery until onions become translucent, about 5 minutes. Sprinkle flour evenly across vegetables and stir until fully incorporated. Continue to cook until mixture thickens into a roux; about 1–2 minutes.

Whisking constantly, pour in hot brown stock and tomato purée. Add garlic, pepper, and bouquet garni. Let simmer, uncovered, for 45 minutes to an hour, stirring occasionally, until sauce is reduced to 3 cups (750 mL). Remove bouquet garni and discard. Keep refrigerated until ready to use.

DEMI-GLACE

*This classical French recipe can be used in Pan-Fried Caribou Steak with Green Peppercorn Sauce (p. 97),
Venison Stir-Fry (p. 95), and Pan-Fried Buffalo Rib Steaks with Blackberry Au Jus (p. 82).
It is essentially an espagnole sauce to which a meat glaze (or* glace de viande*) is added.*

Makes 3 cups (750 mL)

2 tsp canola oil

¼ cup (60 mL) chopped shallots

2 tsp chopped garlic

2 tbsp dry sherry

¼ cup (60 mL) Burgundy wine

4 cups (1 L) brown stock (p. 16)

2 cups (500 mL) Espagnole sauce (p. 19)

¼ tsp salt

1½ tsp coarsely ground black pepper

In a medium saucepan on medium heat, add oil, shallots, and garlic. Sauté until shallots are translucent, about 5 minutes. Add sherry and wine. Continue to simmer until wine is reduced by half. Add brown stock and espagnole sauce, and bring to a boil. Reduce heat to low and simmer for about 40 minutes, until reduced to about 3 cups (750 mL). Season with salt and pepper and let cool. Keep refrigerated until ready to use.

MEAT MARINADE

This marinade is great with for beef roasts and game meats such as elk, moose, deer, and caribou. It can be used in Venison Roulade (p. 94).

Makes 3 cups (750 mL)

½ cup (125 mL) freshly grated horseradish

¼ cup (60 mL) chopped garlic

½ cup (125 mL) coarse salt

½ cup (125 mL) ground black pepper

½ cup (125 mL) grainy Dijon mustard

1 tbsp chopped fresh herbs

¼ cup (60 mL) olive oil

1 tbsp red wine

In a large bowl, combine all ingredients. Rub into meat and marinate for 24 hours in refrigerator.

COURT BOUILLON

Poaching is a healthier cooking method than sautéing or frying in oil, and poaching liquids such as this Court Bouillon infuse fish or poultry with flavor. Use this recipe for Poached Salmon (p. 113).

Makes 6 cups (2 L)

½ large carrot, thinly sliced

½ large onion, thinly sliced

1 celery stalk, thinly sliced

6 whole black peppercorns, crushed

5 fresh parsley stalks

1 bay leaf

1 tbsp salt

¾ cup (185 mL) white wine vinegar

8 cups (2 L) cold fish stock (p. 14) or water

In a large heavy soup pot on high heat, bring all ingredients to a boil. Reduce heat and simmer, uncovered, for 20 minutes. Strain through a fine mesh. Keep refrigerated until ready to use.

FISH VELOUTÉ

This is another "mother sauce" in French cuisine, a versatile base that will allow you to reduce or eliminate the need for heavy cream in cream-based sauces. Some veloutés use chicken stock, but this one incorporates fish.

◀ Makes 4 cups (1 L) ▶

¼ cup (60 mL) butter

¼ cup (60 mL) flour

4 cups (1 L) fish stock (p. 14)

In a small saucepan on medium heat, prepare a blond roux (see below) with butter and flour and allow to cool.

In a large pot on high heat, bring fish stock to a boil. Reduce heat to medium and blend roux into stock. Simmer gently for 20 minutes, stirring frequently. Strain through a fine mesh. Keep refrigerated until ready to use.

MAKING A ROUX

A roux (pronounced "roo") is a thickening agent made from flour and (usually) butter, used extensively in classical French cuisine. The word *roux* means "reddish," but the recipes in this book generally call for a *roux blond* in which the flour and butter are cooked until just golden. Roux can be kept on hand in the refrigerator for up to two weeks, and can be used for thickening stock-based sauces, soups, and stews. *Note:* To reduce your consumption of saturated fats, you may wish to substitute a good quality margarine or use olive oil in place of part of the butter.

1 cup (250 mL) butter (or light olive oil or margarine)

1¾ cups (415 mL) all-purpose flour

In a small saucepan on medium heat, melt butter. Once hot enough that a pinch of flour sprinkled into it will slowly start to bubble, whisk in flour until a thick paste forms. Whisk constantly until it bubbles. After about 15 minutes of continuous cooking and stirring, roux will reach blond stage. Bubbles will start to slow, and the aroma will become nutty or toasty; it should now be golden, very smooth, and thinner than it was.

TOMATO COMPOTE

This makes a delectable accompaniment to any fish dish; try it as an alternative to salsa with mussels (p. 44).

Makes about ½ cup (125 mL)

2 plum tomatoes, blanched and skinned, cut in half

1 tsp olive oil

2 sprigs fresh thyme

4 tbsp olive oil

1 tsp fresh lemon juice

salt, to taste

ground black pepper, to taste

Preheat oven to 225°F (105°C).

Place tomato halves on a parchment-lined cookie sheet. Brush with 1 tsp oil and top with thyme leaves; season with salt and pepper. Bake for 2 hours, until partly dry and soft. Roughly chop tomatoes and place in a bowl. Stir in 4 tbsp oil, lemon juice, salt, and pepper. Will keep in refrigerator for up to 2 days.

BASIL PESTO

Basil pesto is good with Roasted Butternut Squash Ratatouille (p.130).

Makes 6 cups (1.5 L)

4 cups (1 L) fresh basil leaves

¾ cup (185 mL) toasted pine nuts

1 cup (250 mL) chopped fresh garlic

1½ cups (375 mL) olive oil

2 cups (500 mL) freshly grated Parmesan cheese

salt, to taste

ground black pepper, to taste

In a food process or blender, process basil, pine nuts, and garlic until a paste forms. Add oil and cheese and process until smooth. Season with salt and pepper. If not using right away, store in refrigerator for up to 1 week or in freezer for up to 6 months in ice cube trays or small portion containers.

This and the pesto recipes that follow can be used in a variety of sauces, spreads, or stuffings. Follow my suggestions if you like, or get creative and invent your own ways to enjoy these pestos.

DILL PESTO

This pesto is great on most seafood pasta dishes.
I also serve it with Grilled Pacific Salmon (p.115) on baked bannock (p.138).

Makes about 5 cups (1.25 L)

4 cups (1 L) chopped fresh dill

zest of 1 lemon

1 tsp fresh lemon juice

¼ cup (60 mL) toasted pine nuts

2 tbsp chopped garlic

½ cup (125 mL) olive oil

½ cup (125 mL) freshly grated Parmesan cheese

salt, to taste

ground black pepper, to taste

In a food process or blender, process dill, lemon zest and juice, pine nuts, and garlic until a paste forms. Add oil and cheese and process until smooth. Season with salt and pepper. If not using right away, store in refrigerator for up to 1 week or freezer for up to 6 months in ice cube trays or small portion containers.

SAGE PESTO

Sage pesto makes an amazing rub for chicken or turkey (your Thanksgiving bird will thank you if you add it to the dressing); it can also be added to stews or cream sauces. When using the hazelnut variation, I like to serve it with Raspberry Glazed Rabbit Roulade (p.104).

Makes 2 cups (500 mL)

2 cups (500 mL) fresh sage leaves, stems removed

1 tbsp chopped garlic

2 tsp lemon juice

1 tsp lemon zest

¼ cup (60 mL) toasted pine nuts or ½ cup (125 mL) toasted hazelnuts

⅓ cup (80 mL) olive oil

½ cup (125 mL) freshly grated Parmesan cheese

salt, to taste

ground black pepper, to taste

In a food process or blender, process sage, garlic, lemon juice and zest, and pine nuts until a paste forms. Add oil and cheese and process until smooth. Season with salt and pepper. If not using right away, store in refrigerator for up to 1 week or freeze for up to 6 months in ice cube trays or small portion containers.

RED PEPPER PESTO

I like to use this with Braised Buffalo Ribs (p. 84), but it also makes a great pasta sauce.

◀━━━ **Makes about 2 cups (500 mL)** ▶

6 red bell peppers, seeded and quartered

2 tbsp olive oil

2 tbsp chopped garlic

2 cups (500 mL) fresh basil

1 tbsp pine nuts

⅓ cup (80 mL) olive oil

salt, to taste

ground black pepper, to taste

Preheat broiler to high.

Place red peppers on a baking sheet and drizzle with oil. Broil for 20–25 minutes, turning every 5 minutes, until charred. Place in a sealed plastic bag and let sit for 3–5 minutes to steam. Remove and peel off skin; after charring and steaming, it should peel off easily. Set aside.

In a food processor or blender, process garlic until minced. Add basil and pine nuts, and process until smooth. Add roasted red peppers and purée. Drizzle in olive oil and blend again until incorporated. Season with salt and pepper. If not using right away, store in refrigerator for up to 1 week or freeze for up to 6 months in ice cube trays or small portion containers.

FRESH TOMATO SALSA

As an apprentice chef at the Fairmont Chateau in Whistler, BC, one of my regular jobs was to prepare this recipe. It required a lot of cutting because we produced 16-qt/L quantities of this, twice a week, for banquets and the pub. But talk about fresh flavor! Years later, I still make this salsa.

◀ **Makes 4 cups (1 L)** ▶

3 Roma tomatoes, peeled, seeded, and diced

½ cup (125 mL) diced red onions

½ cup (125 mL) diced red bell peppers

½ cup (125 mL) diced green bell peppers

½ cup (125 mL) diced yellow bell peppers

½ cup (125 mL) diced jalapeño peppers

½ cup (125 mL) minced fresh cilantro

2 tsp fresh lime juice

salt, to taste

ground black pepper, to taste

In a medium bowl, combine all ingredients. Season with salt and pepper. Refrigerate for up to 4 hours before serving. Best if refrigerated overnight.

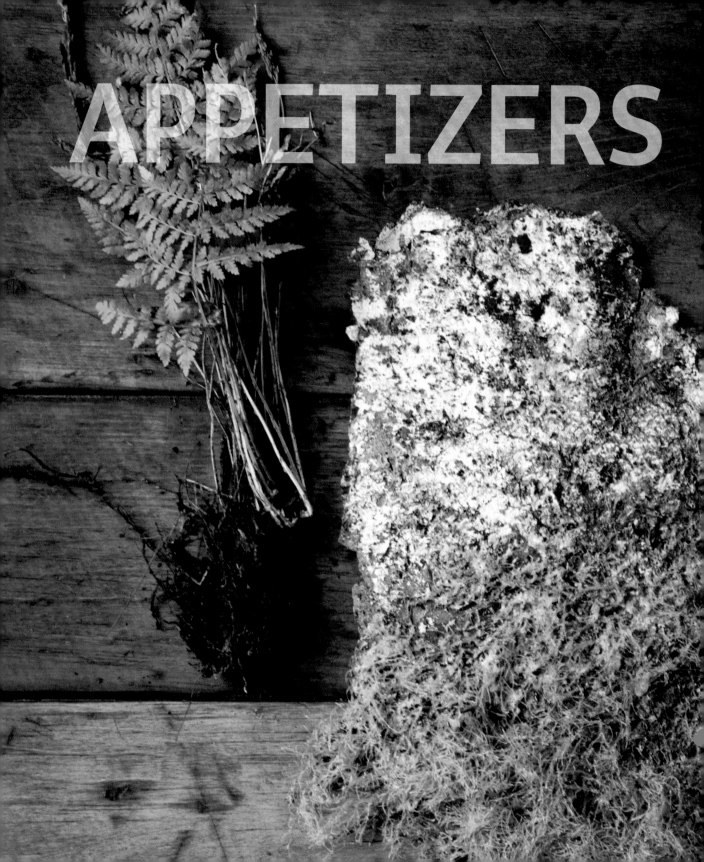

APPETIZERS

SEAWEED-BRINED GRAVLAX

This recipe incorporates both traditional First Nations methods of preserving fish with dried seaweed and the old European way of curing salmon.

2 lb (1 kg) whole wild Pacific salmon, cleaned, pin bones removed (*Tip:* Use tweezers)

4 tbsp coarse sea salt

3 tbsp chopped dried nori (seaweed)

3 tbsp light brown sugar

1 tbsp ground black pepper

4 tbsp chopped fresh dill

3 tbsp vodka

Drape plastic wrap over large glass baking dish. Rinse salmon under cold water and pat dry. Cut salmon in half lengthwise and place one half in dish, skin side down. In a small bowl, combine salt, nori, brown sugar, and pepper. Sprinkle half of mixture over salmon and cover with chopped dill. Pour vodka over mixture.

Spread remaining salt mixture over remaining half of salmon and place on top of salmon in baking dish, skin side up. Fold plastic wrap snuggly around entire salmon. Place pie plate or baking sheet on top of salmon, and add a heavy weight (about 10 lb [4.5 kg]) on top. (*Note:* Clean, foil-wrapped bricks work well, as do large cans of vegetables.) Refrigerate fish for 24–36 hours, turning every 12 hours. Separate fillets and carefully brush off salt, sugar, and dill.

Tip: To make slicing salmon easy, wrap in plastic and place in freezer for about 45 minutes, or until semi-frozen. Remove plastic wrap, and thinly slice at an angle with a sharp knife.

BASIC GRAVLAX

*The First Nations have traditional methods of salting salmon to preserve it.
When I first showed this recipe to introductory pre-apprenticeship culinary students, they didn't want to try
it because it wasn't cooked. Even though it may look raw, the salmon is completely cured through the salting
process—this isn't raw fish! Serve Basic Gravlax on bannock (p. 138), topped with herbed cream cheese,
pickled red onions, capers, and/or salmon caviar.*

2 cups (500 mL) kosher salt

2 tbsp cracked black pepper

½ cup (125 mL) chopped fresh dill

½ cup (125 mL) sugar

zest of 2 oranges

1 8-1b (3.5-kg) wild sockeye salmon, skin on,
pin bones removed (*Tip:* Use tweezers)

In a medium bowl, mix salt, pepper, dill, sugar, and zest. Rinse salmon under cold water and pat dry.

On a clean surface, stretch a length of plastic wrap. Place salmon on top, skin side down. Spread salt mixture evenly over salmon, gently rubbing mixture into flesh. Wrap tightly in plastic wrap and place in a shallow baking dish. Place pie plate or baking sheet on top of salmon, and add a heavy weight (about 10 lb [4.5 kg]) on top. (*Note:* Clean, foil-wrapped bricks work well, as do large cans of vegetables.) Refrigerate for 12 hours. Drain liquid and return to refrigerator. Continue to refrigerate for 12–24 hours, depending on thickness of salmon (the thicker it is, the longer it should marinate).

Carefully unwrap salmon and discard plastic wrap. Scrape off seasoning and rinse salmon under cold running water. Pat dry.

Tip: To make slicing salmon easy, wrap in plastic and place in freezer for about 45 minutes, or until semi-frozen. Remove plastic wrap, and slice at an angle with a sharp knife.

The beets in this recipe give the salmon a vibrant pink color, which makes for a dramatic presentation, whether you are making salmon flowers (see below) or just slicing and arranging them on a plate. Serve on bannock (p. 138), bagels, or crackers, topped with herbed cream cheese, chopped chives, lemon wedges, and capers.

◀ Makes 4 servings ▶

1 large beet, peeled and grated

4 tbsp coarse sea salt

2 tbsp ground black pepper

2 tbsp white sugar

4 tbsp chopped fresh dill

2 lb (1 kg) wild Pacific salmon fillet, skin on, pin bones removed (*Tip:* Use tweezers)

SALMON FLOWERS
For each flower, you'll need five thin slices of gravlax. Roll one up very tightly, starting at the thick end, rolling toward the small end. Roll the second slice around the first, this time beginning at the small end. Let the top drape over so it looks like a flower petal. Repeat with 3 remaining slices.

In a large bowl, combine all ingredients except salmon. Rinse salmon under cold water and pat dry. Place salmon fillet, skin side down, on a long piece of plastic wrap. Spread salt mixture over surface of salmon. Wrap fish tightly and place in a deep baking dish. Place pie plate or baking sheet on top of salmon, and add a heavy weight (about 10 lb [4.5 kg]) on top. (*Note:* Clean, foil-wrapped bricks work well, as do large cans of vegetables.) Place in refrigerator overnight (8 hours). Drain liquid and return to refrigerator for 12–24 hours.

Remove plastic wrap and scrape off salt mixture. Rinse salmon under cold water and pat dry.

Tip: To make slicing salmon easy, wrap in plastic and place in freezer for about 45 minutes, or until semi-frozen. Remove plastic wrap, and thinly slice at an angle with a sharp knife without cutting through skin.

SMOKED SALMON BRUSCHETTA

This was one of the most popular canapés I served when catering the RCMP's 100th anniversary in Surrey, BC, and the opening banquet at the 2010 Winter Olympics in Vancouver. Now you can impress your guests with these tasty appetizers. (Tip: Use plum tomatoes; their skins are thicker and there are fewer seeds and less juice than regular tomatoes.)

◄◄ Makes 6 servings (4 slices per person) ►►

6 or 7 ripe plum tomatoes (about 1½ lb, 750 g)

2 cups (500 mL) chopped smoked wild Pacific salmon

2 tbsp finely chopped red onions

2 garlic cloves, minced

1 tbsp extra-virgin olive oil

1 tsp balsamic vinegar

6–8 fresh basil leaves, chopped

2 tbsp Parmesan cheese

salt, to taste

ground black pepper, to taste

1 baguette French or Italian bread

garlic cloves (for baguette)

¼ cup (60 mL) olive oil (for baguette)

Place top rack in oven close to broiler. Preheat oven to 450°F (230°C).

Blanch tomatoes for 1 minute in boiling water that has just been removed from burner. Drain. Using a sharp, small knife, remove tomato skins. (*Tip:* If tomatoes are too hot, protect your fingertips by rubbing them with an ice cube between cutting tomatoes.) Cut peeled tomatoes in half, and scoop out seeds and juice. Remove stems and cores. Dice tomatoes.

In a large bowl, combine tomatoes, smoked salmon, onions, garlic, oil, and vinegar. Add basil and Parmesan cheese, and season with salt and pepper.

Slice baguette on a diagonal into ½-in (1-cm) thick slices. With a pastry brush, lightly coat one side of each slice with olive oil. Place on baking sheet, olive-oil side down. Toast on top rack of oven for 5–6 minutes, until bread begins to turn golden brown. Or toast bread on griddle for 1 minute per side. With a sharp knife, score each slice 3 times. Rub fresh garlic clove and drizzle ½ tsp olive oil onto each slice.

Place sliced bread on a serving platter, olive oil side up. Top each slice with about 1 tbsp tomato-salmon mixture just before serving, or bread will get soggy. You can also set out bowl of mixture beside bruschetta with a serving spoon so guests can serve themselves.

GRILLED SALMON SKEWERS WITH FRESH DILL SAUCE

Bite-sized pieces of grilled fresh salmon accompanied by a savory pesto-based sauce.

◀ **Makes 4 servings** ▶

1½ lb (750 g) wild Pacific salmon, bones and skin removed, cubed

2 tbsp puréed roasted garlic (below)

2 tbsp chopped fresh dill

2 lemons, juiced and zested

cracked black pepper, to taste

2 tbsp canola oil

¼ cup (60 mL) dill pesto (p. 26)

½ cup (125 mL) white wine

1 cup (250 mL) heavy cream (or whole milk)

salt, to taste

ground black pepper, to taste

Oil broiler or barbecue and preheat to medium. Presoak small bamboo skewers in water.

In a bowl, combine salmon with roasted garlic, dill, lemon juice and zest, pepper, and oil. Marinate for about 15 minutes. Spear 3 cubes of salmon onto each presoaked skewer. Grill or broil for 2 minutes per side. Remove and set aside.

In a medium frying pan on medium-low heat, bring dill pesto and wine to a simmer until reduced by half. Add cream and reduce by half again. Drizzle dill sauce over skewers. Season with salt and pepper.

ROASTED GARLIC
Preheat oven to 375°F (190°C). Toss 12 cloves of garlic in 1 tsp olive oil. Roast in oven for 15 minutes.

HOT SMOKED TROUT

I used to make this in a smokehouse; now I use it to teach my culinary students about the art of smoking fish. You will need a smoker for this recipe, and some woodchips to give your fish a smoky flavor. Serve as a light main course on a bed of dressed dandelion greens or as an appetizer with Horseradish Cream (p. 109).

◀━━━ Makes 4 servings as a main; 8 as an appetizer ▶

½ cup (125 mL) kosher salt

4 cups (1 L) water

6–8 4–6-oz (115 g–175-g) trout fillets, skin on, pin bones removed (*Tip*: Use tweezers)

In a 4-quart (4-L) container, combine salt and water and stir until salt has dissolved, 1–2 minutes. Add trout fillets, making sure they are submerged. Cover and refrigerate for 3 hours.

Remove trout from brine. Rinse thoroughly and pat dry. Place trout, skin side down, on cooling rack set in a baking pan. Refrigerate uncovered for about 24 hours, until skin becomes shiny and somewhat sticky.

Adjust smoker temperature to 150–160°F (65–70°C). Place trout onto racks, skin side down, separated by about ¼ in (6 mm). Place in smoker. Smoke for 2½–3 hours, or until fish is cooked through, darkened in color, and has desired smoke flavor.

MAPLE-GLAZED PACIFIC SARDINES

At the national conference for the Canadian Culinary Federation in 2011, these sardines were a hit. Serve them on slices of baked bannock or bread.

Makes 4 servings

8 whole Pacific sardines, filleted

1 tsp ground dill seeds

2 tbsp white sugar

2 tbsp kosher salt

3 tbsp olive oil

2 tbsp finely chopped garlic

4 tbsp chopped fresh dill

2 tbsp maple syrup

6 slices baked bannock (p. 138)

2 tbsp maple syrup, for garnish

2 fresh lemons, cut into wedges, for garnish

Preheat broiler to medium-high.

In a large glass baking dish, sprinkle sardine fillets with dill seeds, sugar, and salt and let stand in refrigerator for 1–2 hours. Rinse off under cold water, and pat sardines dry with paper towels. Place sardines on a broiling pan and brush them, skin side up, with olive oil. Brush with 1 tbsp maple syrup. Sprinkle with chopped garlic and fresh dill. Broil skin side up for 1 minute. Turn, and brush sardines with remaining syrup. Broil until golden brown, about 1 minute. Place sardines on baked bannock or slices of toasted bread, and drizzle with more maple syrup. Squeeze lemon juice over fish.

CLAM FRITTERS

Serve these crispy bites with Dill Sauce and/or Lime Cayenne Dip (recipes below).

◄◼ Makes 6–8 servings ◼►

1 cup (250 mL) shelled and chopped baby clams, juice reserved

1 medium onion, finely diced

1 celery stalk, finely diced

½ cup (125 mL) dried chopped nori (seaweed)

1 tsp curry powder

2 tbsp chopped fresh dill

3 cups (750 mL) all-purpose flour

4 tsp baking powder

2 eggs, beaten

salt, to taste

ground black pepper, to taste

Preheat a deep fryer to 350°F (180°C).
Note: A healthier alternative is to cook fritters in a cast-iron frying pan with minimal oil on medium-low heat, like a pancake.

In a small bowl, mix clams, onions, celery, seaweed, curry powder, and dill, and set aside. In a large bowl, mix flour, baking powder, eggs, salt, pepper, and reserved clam juice. Stir in clam mixture. Let batter rest for 1 hour. Using 2 tablespoons, scoop batter and carefully drop dollop into hot oil in deep fryer or frying pan. Cook until golden brown. Repeat until all batter has been used up.

DILL SAUCE
Makes 1 cup (250mL)

1 cup (250 mL) low-fat mayonnaise

1 tbsp white wine vinegar

2 tbsp fresh chopped dill

1 tsp fresh lemon juice

salt, to taste

ground white pepper, to taste

In a large bowl, mix all ingredients.

LIME CAYENNE DIP
Makes 1 cup (250ml)

1 cup (250 mL) low-fat mayonnaise

1 tbsp white wine vinegar

1 tsp fresh cayenne pepper

2 tsp fresh lime juice

salt, to taste

ground white pepper, to taste

In a small bowl, mix all ingredients.
This dip is best if made the day before.

OYSTERS ROCKEFELLER (FIRST NATIONS STYLE)

I use this recipe to teach Aboriginal students a classical method of preparing seafood. Using stinging nettles, dandelion greens, or sorrel instead of traditional spinach, gives a new twist to this dish.

◀ Makes 12 oysters ▶

(2–6 servings, depending on how large they are and much your guests like oysters)

¼ cup (60 mL) unsalted butter

1 celery stalk, finely sliced

2 green onions, finely sliced

1 garlic clove, finely minced

1 tbsp finely chopped parsley

1 cup (250 mL) finely chopped stinging nettles,
   dandelion greens, or sorrel leaves

dash Pernod, or other anise-flavored liqueur

2 slices fresh white bread, crusts removed,
   torn into pieces

12 fresh oysters in shell

1 tbsp Pernod

rock salt, for serving

12 lemon wedges, for garnish

12 parsley sprigs, for garnish

salt, to taste

Tabasco sauce, to taste

Preheat broiler to high.

In a large frying pan, melt butter and sauté celery, onions, garlic, parsley, greens, and dash of Pernod. Stir constantly for about 3 minutes. Remove from heat.

In a food processor or blender, combine greens mixture with bread and process for about 30 seconds. Using an oyster knife, twist open shells and remove oysters. (Note: Take care when opening oysters; protect your hand by wearing an oyster glove or covering knife with a towel.) In a large bowl, toss oysters with 1 tbsp Pernod. Drain oysters and reserve liquid. Remove any shell fragments. Discard top shells, clean and dry bottom shells.

Line a baking tray with rock salt and place oyster shells on top. Place 1 oyster into each shell and spoon reserved liquid onto each. Spoon crumb mixture on top, completely covering each oyster. Broil for 1–2 minutes, until topping bubbles. Arrange oysters on a serving dish and garnish with sprigs of parsley and lemon wedges. Season oysters to taste with salt and/or Tabasco sauce.

Clockwise from bottom left: Oysters Rockefeller, Lime Cayenne Dip (p. 41), Clam Fritters (p. 41)

MUSSELS WITH FRESH TOMATO SALSA

You can use clams instead of mussels in this recipe. Serve with toasted baguette or bannock slices (p. 138). This is also good with Tomato Compote (p. 24) instead of the salsa.

◀ **Makes 6 servings** ▶

5 dozen fresh mussels

1 tbsp olive oil

¼ cup (60 mL) chopped green onions

2 garlic cloves, minced

½ cup (125 mL) white wine

4 large ripe plum tomatoes, peeled and
   roughly chopped

1 tsp dried oregano

¼ cup (60 mL) chopped cilantro or parsley

3 cups (750 mL) fresh tomato salsa (p. 29)

1 cup (250 mL) freshly grated Parmesan cheese,
   to garnish

Clean and debeard mussels and set aside. In a large saucepan on medium heat, sauté oil, green onions, and garlic for 1 minute. Add mussels and white wine. Cover and steam for 4–5 minutes, until shells open. Add tomatoes, oregano, and cilantro. Detach mussels from shell, but serve them on the half shell. Spoon salsa onto each mussel and place on platter. Sprinkle with Parmesan cheese.

JALAPEÑO PRAWNS

This is a very simple yet tasty starter that I learned at the Avenue Grill restaurant, where I started my culinary apprenticeship.

◄ Makes 4 servings ►

20 large whole prawns

1 cup (250 mL) all-purpose flour

1 tsp salt

1 tsp ground black pepper

1 fresh jalapeño pepper, chopped and seeded

1 tbsp canola oil

¼ cup (60 mL) white wine

2 tbsp fresh lime juice

2 tbsp butter, softened

¼ cup (60 mL) minced fresh cilantro, for garnish

Remove heads from prawns, then clean and devein. When removing shells, leave tail intact. In a large bowl, combine flour, salt, pepper, and jalapeño peppers. Dredge prawns in seasoned flour and shake off excess.

In a large frying pan on medium-high, heat oil to smoking point. Sauté for 3–4 minutes per side, or until they turn bright pink. Deglaze pan with white wine and lime juice. Remove from heat. Stir in butter, and garnish with cilantro.

SPOT PRAWN RICE ROLL

This recipe combines Asian flavors and technique with a coastal First Nations essential, the prawn. Here I use the spot prawn, a BC delicacy in the spring, but you can use any fresh variety. Serve with Spicy Dipping Sauce (opposite).

◄■ **Makes 12 rolls** ■►

2 lb (1 kg) fresh spot prawns

2 garlic cloves, minced

1 tbsp minced fresh ginger

juice of 1 lime

1 tsp soy sauce

½ head iceberg lettuce, thinly sliced

¼ cup (60 mL) chopped mint leaves

¼ cup (60 mL) chopped basil leaves

12 green onions, julienned

6 carrots, peeled and julienned

3 cups (750 mL) rice vermicelli

2 tbsp oyster sauce

¼ cup (60 mL) chopped cilantro

1 cup (250 mL) peanuts (optional)

1 tsp canola oil (optional)

12 rice paper wraps

1 cup (250 mL) sweet chili sauce

1 cup (250 mL) Hoisin sauce

In a large pot filled with water on high heat, boil prawns for about 3–6 minutes, until shells turn bright red, but don't overcook. Remove from pot. Peel shrimp and chop. In a large bowl, combine garlic, ginger, lime juice, and soy sauce. Add prawns and set aside. Place lettuce, mint, basil, green onions, and carrots on a platter and cover with wet paper towel. Set aside.

In a large pot on high, cook vermicelli in boiling water for 1 minute. Drain and allow to cool. Stir in oyster sauce, cilantro, and lime juice and set aside. (Optional: In a small frying pan on high heat, fry peanuts in canola oil for 2 minutes. Let cool, then add to vermicelli mixture.)

Rehydrate rice paper by soaking in water for about 45–60 seconds. On a clean surface, lay out rice paper. Place 4 tbsp shrimp, vermicelli, and vegetables on each wrapper, and add 4 tsp each sweet chili and Hoisin sauce. Roll wrappers up.

Bonito flakes are dried, shaved bonito fish (skipjack mackerel) that add a savory flavor to Japanese foods.

SPICY DIPPING SAUCE

Makes about 1 ½ cups (625mL)

⅛ cup (30 mL) fish sauce

2 cups (500 mL) water

4 tbsp chili flakes

4 tbsp bonito flakes

1 lime, juiced and zested

In a large saucepan, bring all ingredients to a boil.

Let cook for 5 minutes. Remove from heat, cool, and strain.

VENISON & CARAMELIZED ONION TARTS

This is great-tasting finger food and easy to make (the shells are pre-made). Venison loin is lean and tender, and the juniper berries add a citrus-like tang.

◄ Makes 8 tarts ►

2 tbsp olive oil

4 red onions, thinly sliced

2 tbsp brown sugar

½ tsp chopped fresh sage

½ tsp chopped fresh rosemary

1 tbsp balsamic vinegar

salt, to taste

ground black pepper, to taste

8 4-in (10-cm) frozen tart shells

dried beans (to fill tart shells)

1 lb (500 g) venison short loin

1 tsp Dijon mustard

½ tsp cracked black pepper

½ tsp chopped dried juniper berries

salt, to taste

ground black pepper, to taste

8 sprigs fresh rosemary, for garnish

Preheat oven to 350°F (180°C).

In a large frying pan on medium, heat olive oil. Add onions, brown sugar, sage, and rosemary. Sauté for about 4 minutes, then add balsamic vinegar. Season with salt and pepper. Remove from heat and allow to cool. Can be refrigerated for up to 1 week.

Line tart shells with foil and fill with dried beans. Bake for 20 minutes. ("Blind" baking them like this prevents shells from shrinking.) Remove beans and discard foil. Allow shells to cool.

Remove silver membrane from venison short loin. Rub with mustard, pepper, and juniper berries, and season with salt and pepper. In a large frying pan on medium-high heat, sear venison for 3–4 minutes on each side.

Place venison in a 10-in (25-cm) roasting pan and bake for 20 minutes (for medium rare). Remove and let stand for 10 minutes before thinly slicing.

Fill tart shells with caramelized onions and top with sliced venison. Garnish with sprigs of fresh rosemary.

SALADS

& SALAD

DRESSINGS

ROASTED CORN & WILD RICE SALAD

This is a great summer salad with a nutty flavor and a sweet-and-sour dressing.

◄ Makes 4 servings ►

4 ears fresh corn, husks removed

1 tbsp olive oil (for corn)

salt, to taste (for corn)

ground black pepper, to taste (for corn)

3 cups (750 mL) cooked and cooled wild rice

½ cup (125 mL) diced roasted red bell peppers

1 cup (250 mL) diced celery

2 cups (500 mL) diced red onions

¼ cup (60 mL) chopped parsley

salt, to taste

ground black pepper, to taste

MAPLE VINAIGRETTE

2 tbsp olive oil

1 tbsp cider vinegar

1½ tsp Dijon mustard

2 tsp maple syrup

Oil broiler or barbecue and preheat to high. In a large pot, bring salted water to a boil. Blanch corn for about 5 minutes. Remove from water and place in ice-water bath to stop cooking. Season corn with olive oil and salt and pepper to taste. Place on barbecue or in broiler for 2–3 minutes per side. Let cool and cut corn from cob.

For the vinaigrette:
In a small bowl, combine all ingredients.

In another bowl, combine all salad ingredients, and toss with vinaigrette. Season with salt and pepper to taste.

WATERCRESS SALAD WITH MUSTARD WALNUT DRESSING

I made this salad with Aboriginal students for a banquet at the Institut de tourisme et d'hôtellerie du Québec in Montreal.

◀◀ Makes 4 servings ▶▶

½ cup (125 mL) coarse fresh breadcrumbs

2 tbsp olive oil

salt, to taste

ground black pepper, to taste

1 lb (500 g) king trumpet or cremini mushrooms, very thinly sliced

2 small red onions, very thinly sliced into rings

2 cups (500 mL) watercress leaves and tender stems

½ cup (125 mL) Mustard Walnut Dressing (see below)

MUSTARD WALNUT DRESSING
This dressing is best if allowed to sit refrigerated overnight.

1 cup (250 mL) chopped walnuts

2 tbsp olive oil

1½ tbsp red wine vinegar

1½ tbsp Pommery mustard

2 garlic cloves, minced

salt, to taste

ground black pepper, to taste

In a small frying pan on medium-high heat, combine breadcrumbs and oil. Sauté, stirring frequently, until breadcrumbs are golden brown, 4–5 minutes. Season with salt and pepper and transfer to a paper-towel-lined plate. Let cool.

For the dressing:
In a small bowl, whisk together all ingredients.

In a large serving bowl, combine mushrooms, onions, and watercress. Toss to coat with dressing. Divide among 4 plates and sprinkle with breadcrumbs.

WARM DANDELION GREENS SALAD

This recipe is a twist on one of my old favorites, warm spinach salad.

◀ **Makes 4 servings** ▶

10 cups (2.5 L) organic dandelion leaves

2 tbsp olive oil

1 tbsp red wine vinegar

½ tsp salt

ground black pepper, to taste

6 slices smoked bacon, chopped

1 slice French or Italian bread, cubed

2 tbsp red wine vinegar (for dressing)

1 hard-boiled egg, crumbled

Wash greens and tear into small pieces, discarding tough stems. In a warm salad bowl, mix greens with oil and 1 tbsp vinegar. Sprinkle with salt and pepper and lightly toss.

In a large frying pan on medium heat, fry bacon until half cooked. Add bread cubes, and fry until cubes are golden brown and bacon is cooked. Drain fat from pan and pat bacon with paper towel to absorb excess fat. Toss greens with bacon and croutons.

In a small saucepan on high heat, bring vinegar to a boil. Once bubbling, pour onto greens and toss. Top with crumbled egg.

SMOKED TROUT SALAD

I grew up eating smoked trout with boiled potatoes; this is a new take on a traditional recipe.
You can make your own smoked trout or find it at a good fishmonger.

Makes 2 servings

4 oz (115 g) skinned smoked trout fillet, flaked (p. 39)

¼ cup (60 mL) minced celery

2 tbsp minced shallot

2 tbsp low-fat mayonnaise

2 tbsp reduced-fat sour cream

1 tsp freshly grated lemon zest

2 tbsp lemon juice

1 tbsp minced fresh dill, or 1 tsp dried

½ tsp ground black pepper

2 cups (500 mL) mixed salad greens

8 small heirloom tomatoes, sliced in half

In a medium bowl, combine trout, celery, shallots, mayonnaise, sour cream, lemon zest and juice, dill, and pepper. Arrange salad greens and tomatoes on 2 plates, and top with trout mixture.

MARINATED SALMON SALAD

The SuperChefs kids and I prepare this summer salad at public events and always receive rave reviews.

◄ Makes 4 servings ►

1 lb (500 g) boneless wild Pacific salmon fillet, pin bones removed (*Tip*: Use tweezers)

1 cup (250 mL) fresh dandelion greens, watercress, or arugula

¼ cup (60 mL) lemon juice

¼ cup (60 mL) extra-virgin olive oil

1½ tbsp toasted fennel seeds

¼ cup (60 mL) chopped fresh dill

sea salt, to taste

ground black pepper, to taste

1 bulb fennel, thinly sliced, for garnish

½ red onion, thinly sliced, for garnish

Remove skin and brown flesh beneath skin from salmon with a sharp knife. Slice salmon very thinly, at a diagonal, and lay in a glass pan or plate.

In a small bowl, whisk together lemon juice, oil, and toasted fennel seeds. Add dill and pour half of mixture over sliced salmon. Cover and refrigerate for up to 3 hours to marinate. The salmon should change color from bright red to pale pink. Toss remaining marinade with greens. Season with salt and pepper. Add to plate of marinated salmon, and garnish with thinly sliced fennel and red onion.

NIÇOISE SALAD WITH POACHED SALMON

When I teach this recipe in the SuperChefs program, I like to emphasize the local, fresh ingredients and promote healthy cooking to the students. This Niçoise uses salmon instead of the traditional tuna.

◀■ Makes 4 servings ■▶

½ lb (250 g) baby new potatoes

1 cup (250 mL) chopped green beans

4 4-oz (460-g) poached salmon fillets (p. 113)

4 cups (1 L) court bouillon (p. 22)

½ lb (250 g) mixed baby greens

¼ cup (60 mL) artichokes, cooked and quartered (with bristly "choke" section removed), or canned

½ cup (125 mL) halved cherry tomatoes

¼ cup (60 mL) pitted black olives

4 eggs, hard-boiled, sliced into quarters

VINAIGRETTE

⅛ cup (30 mL) white wine vinegar

2 tsp Dijon mustard

1 garlic clove, minced

1 shallot, finely chopped

½ cup (125 mL) canola oil

1 tsp honey

In a large pot, boil or steam potatoes for about 15–20 minutes, until tender. In a large pot fitted with a steamer on high heat, steam green beans for 1 minute. Place in cold-water bath to cool. Poach salmon in court bouillon for 10 minutes. Set aside to cool.

For the vinaigrette:
In a medium bowl, combine ingredients and stir to combine well.

In a large salad bowl, assemble potatoes, green beans, salmon, greens, artichokes, tomatoes, olives, and eggs. Spoon vinaigrette over salad.

Clockwise from top left:
Curried Dandelion Greens
with Caramelized Onions and
Cashews (p. 126), Niçoise Salad
with Poached Smoked Salmon,
Lemon Poppyseed Dressing
(p. 65)

SEA ASPARAGUS SALAD WITH SEARED PACIFIC SEAFOOD & SEAWEED VINAIGRETTE

Also known as "sea beans," Salicornia (sea asparagus) is a salt-tolerant plant that grows on beaches and salt marshes. It has a salty taste, and its flavor and texture are like asparagus. It beautifully complements the flavor of the fish.

◀ **Makes 4 servings** ▶

2 cups (500 mL) fresh sea asparagus

8 3–4 oz (90–115 g) fresh halibut cheeks

8 large sea scallops

8 large spot prawns

salt, to taste

freshly cracked black pepper, to taste

½ cup (125 mL) powdered nori (seaweed)

2 tbsp olive oil

2 heirloom tomatoes

½ cup (125 mL) ripe cherry tomatoes

1 small red onion, diced

½ lb (250 g) ripe figs, quartered

½ cup (125 mL) chopped fresh basil

2 cups (500 mL) watercress

2 cups (500 mL) mixed baby greens

SEAWEED VINAIGRETTE

2 tbsp chopped nori

1 cup (250 mL) canola oil

1 tbsp wasabi powder

1½ tbsp lemon juice

1 tbsp rice vinegar

1 tbsp Dijon mustard

2 tbsp light soy sauce

1 tsp white sugar

salt, to taste

Clean sea asparagus in fresh water and remove brownish sections. Set aside. In a large saucepan on high heat, bring water to a boil. Add sea asparagus and cook for 3 minutes. Remove asparagus with a slotted spoon, and submerge in large bowl of ice and water. Once cooled, drain well and transfer to a serving bowl.

Pat seafood dry with paper towels and season with salt and pepper. Dredge in powdered seaweed.

In a large frying pan on medium, heat olive oil. Place seafood in skillet and cook for about 2–3 minutes per side, depending on size. (Don't overcrowd the pan; fry in batches if necessary.) Remove seafood, place on paper-towel-covered plate, and set aside.

For the vinaigrette:
In a bowl, soak nori in enough water to cover for about 5 minutes, until softened. Drain and discard water. In a medium bowl, whisk together remaining ingredients for dressing, adding nori once combined.

Add tomatoes, onion, figs, basil, watercress, and baby greens to sea asparagus. Dress with all but 4 tbsp vinaigrette and toss to mix well. Arrange on 4 salad plates, with seafood placed in center of salad. Drizzle with remainder of vinaigrette.

BARBECUED PACIFIC SEAFOOD SALAD WITH POMMERY MUSTARD DRESSING

Mustard dressing on seafood? Boy, does it work!
Alternately, you could also try the Balsamic Vinaigrette (p. 64) on this salad.

◀ Makes 4 servings ▶

10 mussels

8 clams

8 Pacific prawns

4 whole calamari, cleaned and scored

½ tsp chopped garlic

1 tsp lemon juice

salt, to taste

ground black pepper, to taste

6 tbsp olive oil

¼ cup (60 mL) diced red onions

1 red bell pepper, quartered

salt, to taste

ground black pepper, to taste

½ tbsp olive oil

¼ cup (60 mL) Pommery Mustard Dressing (opposite)

1 tbsp chopped fresh parsley, for garnish

2 tbsp chopped fresh chives, for garnish

Oil barbecue or grill and preheat to medium.

In a large bowl, combine mussels, clams, prawns, and calamari, and season with garlic, lemon juice, salt, pepper, and 6 tbsp olive oil. In a separate bowl, combine onions and bell peppers, and season with salt, pepper, and ½ tbsp olive oil.

Barbecue or grill mussels and clams just until open. Remove mussels and clams from heat, and grill prawns and calamari for about 4–6 minutes per side. Remove from heat. Grill vegetables for 3–4 minutes per side, giving them a cross-hatch.

Prepare the dressing.

In a large serving bowl, combine all ingredients. Toss with dressing and garnish with parsley and chives.

POMMERY MUSTARD DRESSING

1 cup (250 mL) canola oil
¼ cup (60 mL) red wine vinegar
1½ tbsp lemon juice
2 tbsp grainy Pommery Dijon mustard
1 tbsp lemon juice
1 tsp sugar
salt, to taste
ground black pepper, to taste

In a blender, process all ingredients for 30 seconds.

Pommery Moutarde de Lion is
a whole-grain mustard made in
France in 1632.

BALSAMIC VINAIGRETTE

This is a basic staple dressing that complements any salad in this book. It can be used on the Barbecued Pacific Seafood Salad (p. 62) instead of the Pommery Mustard Dressing.

◀ Makes 1 cup (250 mL) ▶

¾ cup (185 mL) extra-virgin olive oil

⅓ cup (80 mL) balsamic vinegar

1 tbsp lemon juice

1 tsp Dijon mustard

1 garlic clove, minced

¼ tsp salt

¼ tsp ground black pepper

In a small bowl, whisk all ingredients together until well combined.

LEMON POPPY SEED DRESSING

Serve this dressing over any of the seafood salads in this book. I especially like it with Niçoise Salad (instead of the vinaigrette).

Makes 1 cup (250 mL)

⅓ cup (80 mL) olive oil

⅓ cup (80 mL) canola oil

5 tbsp white sugar

⅓ cup (80 mL) fresh lemon juice

2 tsp chopped shallots

1 tsp Dijon mustard

1 tbsp poppy seeds

salt, to taste

ground black pepper, to taste

In a blender, process the oils, sugar, lemon juice, shallots, and mustard on medium-high for 1 minute. Stir in poppy seeds, and season with salt and pepper.

SOUPS

BUTTERNUT SQUASH VEGETABLE SOUP

This is a delicious, healthy, vegetarian-friendly soup that will warm body and soul on cold, dreary days.

Makes 4 servings

2 butternut squash, peeled and cut into
    1-in (2.5-cm) cubes

1 head cauliflower, cut into florets

1 onion, diced

2 tbsp margarine

2 medium zucchini, diced

1 cup (250 mL) chicken stock (p. 15) or
    vegetable stock

½ tsp salt

In a double boiler or a large pot fitted with a removable steamer on high heat, steam squash for 20 minutes, until tender. Add cauliflower florets to steam for last 5 minutes.

In a large pot on medium heat, sauté onions in margarine for about 7 minutes until lightly browned, then add zucchini, stock, and salt. Bring to a boil, and add squash and cauliflower. Reduce heat and cook for 20 minutes.

In a blender or with an immersion blender, purée soup. *Caution:* Be careful when blending hot liquids! Return puréed soup to pot on low and simmer, about 5 minutes.

TUSCAN WHITE BEAN SOUP

This is one of my favorite soups. It's simple but flavorful and filling. Using vegetable stock instead of chicken makes for a hearty vegetarian meal.

Makes 4 servings

¾ cup (185 mL) dried white beans, soaked in cold water overnight

2 tbsp olive oil

2 large onions, diced

1 fennel bulb, chopped

4 celery stalks, chopped

2 parsnips, diced

4 cups (1 L) chicken stock (p. 15) or vegetable stock

salt, to taste

ground black pepper, to taste

2 tsp fresh tarragon, for garnish

1 tbsp olive oil, for garnish

Drain soaked beans and discard liquid. In a large pot on high heat, boil beans rapidly in 2 cups (500 mL) water for 10 minutes. Drain. Cover beans with 2 cups fresh water, and simmer on medium-low heat for 1–2 hours, until soft.

In a heavy saucepan on medium, heat oil and sauté onions, fennel, celery, and parsnips for 3 minutes. Add cooked beans and stock to saucepan. Continue to simmer until vegetables are tender. In a blender or with an immersion blender, purée soup. *Caution:* Be careful when blending hot liquids! Return puréed soup to pot on low and simmer, about 5 minutes. Season with salt and pepper to taste. Garnish soup with fresh tarragon and olive oil.

POTATO & LEEK SOUP

Growing up, we made a recipe similar to this one with moose or rabbit broth. While it's a very simple recipe, its warmth was enough to sustain us during the cold winter months.

◄ **Makes 4 servings** ►

½ cup (125 mL) chopped cooked bacon

3 tbsp butter

1 cup (250 mL) chopped leeks, white part only

1 tsp minced garlic

3 cups (750 mL) diced potatoes

6 cups (1.5 L) chicken stock (p. 15) or
    white wine sauce (p. 118)

1 bay leaf

salt, to taste

ground black pepper, to taste

¼ cup (60 mL) 35% cream (optional), for garnish

chopped chives, for garnish

In a soup pot on medium heat, cook bacon in 1 tsp of water for about 3 minutes, allowing water to evaporate. Add butter, leeks, and garlic, and cook for 3–4 minutes, until leeks are translucent. Add potatoes, stock, and bay leaf, and bring to a boil. Reduce heat to low and simmer for about 30 minutes.

Remove soup from heat and discard bay leaf. In a food processor or blender, purée until smooth. Strain through a fine sieve. Season with salt and pepper to taste, and garnish with cream and chives.

CREAM OF MUSHROOM SOUP

I love cream of mushroom soup. Adding the woodsy taste of wild varieties to this comforting, creamy soup makes it even better.

◀ **Makes 6 servings** ▶

6 cups (1.5 L) chanterelle (or oyster, morel, or shaggy mane) mushrooms, chopped

4 tbsp canola oil

8 tbsp butter

1 medium onion, diced

4 garlic cloves, minced

1 tsp salt

¼ tsp ground white pepper

8 tbsp all-purpose flour

3 cups (750 mL) low-fat milk

3 cups (750 mL) chicken stock (p. 15)

In a medium saucepan on medium heat, sauté mushrooms in oil for about 45 seconds. Remove from heat and set aside. Add butter, onions, garlic, salt, and pepper and sauté until onions are translucent, about 5 minutes. Stir in flour and cook for about 2 minutes. Gradually add stock, 1 cup at a time, using a whisk to stir so soup doesn't get lumpy. Gradually whisk in milk, using same method as for stock. Simmer for 10 minutes. Add sautéed mushrooms to soup.

CORN CHOWDER

In the fall, when the sweet corn of British Columbia's Fraser Valley is ripe, I serve this delicious and sweet-tasting chowder with freshly baked corn bread (p. 137).

Makes 6 servings

1 cup (250 mL) diced onions

½ cup (125 mL) diced celery

1 tbsp minced garlic

2 tbsp butter or olive oil

2 tbsp all-purpose flour

8 cups (2 L) vegetable stock or chicken stock (p. 15), heated

2 potatoes, diced

½ cup (125 mL) diced carrots

½ cup (125 mL) diced green bell peppers

4 ears fresh corn kernels

½ cup (125 mL) whipping cream (or low-fat milk)

1 tbsp chopped fresh dill

1 tbsp chopped fresh parsley

In a medium pot on medium heat, sauté onions, celery, and garlic in butter, until onions are translucent, about 5 minutes. Stir in flour, creating a roux (see p. 23). Pour in heated stock, one ladle at a time, stirring constantly so flour does not get lumpy. Add vegetables. Slowly simmer until vegetables are tender but not mushy. Remove from heat and stir in cream, dill, and parsley.

SEAFOOD CHOWDER

This rich and delicious chowder was a favorite with my customers at the Toody Ni Grill.
The recipe below features a few modifications and additions that make it even better than it was.
Note: *Use margarine or olive oil instead of bacon fat or butter for a healthier soup,*
or use just 1 tbsp bacon fat for flavor and a scant ½ cup olive oil.

◀▬ **Makes 6–8 servings as a main course** ▬▶

8 cups (2 L) fish stock (p. 14) or water

½ cup (125 mL) bacon fat or butter

1 medium onion, diced

1 celery stalk, diced

4 garlic cloves, crushed

1 bay leaf

1 cup (250 mL) white wine

½ cup (125 mL) all-purpose flour

1 (125 g) large potato, diced

1 medium carrot, diced

½ green bell pepper, diced

⅓ lb (170 g) fresh clams

⅓ lb (170 g) cubed wild Pacific salmon

⅓ lb (170 g) cubed red snapper

salt, to taste

ground black pepper, to taste

about ½ cup (125 mL) whipping cream

2 tbsp chopped fresh dill

2 tbsp chopped fresh parsley

In a large saucepan on high heat, bring stock to a boil then reduce heat to a simmer. In a large heavy soup pot on medium-high, melt bacon fat or butter. Add onions, celery, garlic, and bay leaf, and sauté until onions are translucent, about 5 minutes. Add white wine and simmer until reduced by half. Whisk in flour and cook, stirring constantly, for about 2 minutes (making a roux, see p. 23).

Slowly add hot stock to roux, stirring well to prevent lumps, and bring to a simmer. Add potatoes, carrots, and bell peppers and simmer until vegetables are tender. Add clams, salmon, and red snapper. Cook on low heat for about 10 minutes, until fish is cooked through and tender. Discard bay leaf. Season with salt and pepper. Remove from heat and stir in just enough cream to turn chowder white. Stir in fresh dill and parsley just before serving.

CLAM CHOWDER

I first made this chowder during my apprenticeship at the Avenue Grill in Vancouver's Kerrisdale neighborhood. Clam chowder is often served in our traditional Feast (Potlatch) Hall.

◄ Makes 4–6 servings ►

¼ lb (125 g) sliced fresh side pork (or bacon)

½ cup (125 mL) chopped onions

½ cup (125 mL) chopped celery

½ cup (125 mL) pastry flour

6 cups (1.5 L) fish stock (p. 14)

2¼ cups (530 mL) clam nectar

1 bouquet garni (p. 14)

½ cup (125 mL) diced potatoes

28-oz (796-mL) can baby clams with nectar

1 cup (250 mL) 35% cream (or ½ cup [125 mL] evaporated milk) (optional)

salt, to taste

ground black pepper, to taste

In a large pot on medium-high heat, brown pork or bacon. Add onions and celery, and sauté until translucent, about 5 minutes. Whisk in flour and stir constantly until dissolved, to make a very light roux (p. 23). Whisk in fish stock and clam nectar, and add bouquet garni. Simmer for 1 minute, then add potatoes and simmer for 20 minutes, until tender. Stir in baby clams and nectar and simmer for about 5 minutes more. Stir in cream and adjust seasoning to taste. Remove bouquet garni before serving.

RABBIT NOODLE SOUP

We used to get our rabbits from the Wet'suwet'en territories in British Columbia, where this recipe is sometimes called "medicine in a bowl." Whether you use rabbit or substitute chicken, this soup is healthy and comforting on a cold winter day. Serve with baked bannock (p. 138).

◀■ Makes 6–8 servings ■▶

2 cups (500 mL) cubed rabbit (or boneless, skinless, cubed chicken breasts)

8 cups (2 L) rabbit (or chicken) stock (p. 15)

½ cup (125 mL) diced onions

½ cup (125 mL) diced celery

½ cup (125 mL) diced carrots

2 tbsp olive oil

2 garlic cloves, minced

½ cup (125 mL) diced zucchini

½ cup (125 mL) diced green bell peppers

1 bouquet garni (p. 14)

1 cup (250 mL) Homemade Pasta (p. 143) or dried (e.g., macaroni, rotini, penne)

salt, to taste

ground black pepper, to taste

chopped fresh parsley, for garnish

In a stock pot on high heat, bring rabbit and stock to a boil. Reduce heat to medium and simmer until tender, about 20 minutes.

Meanwhile, in a large frying pan, sauté onions, celery, and carrots in oil until translucent, about 5 minutes. Add garlic, zucchini, and bell peppers and sauté for about 5 more minutes. Add vegetable mixture and bouquet garni to stock and continue to simmer.

In a large saucepan of water, cook pasta until al dente (still somewhat firm) and add to soup. Season soup to taste. Remove bouquet garni before serving and garnish with parsley.

VENISON BEAN SOUP

This hearty and warming soup is a variation of one often served in our Feast (Potlatch) Halls.

◀■ Makes 4–6 servings ■▶

2 tbsp olive oil

1¾ lb (875 g) venison, diced into 1-in (2.5-cm) cubes

6 cups (1.5 L) venison or beef stock (p. 18)

1 cup (250 mL) diced carrots

1 cup (250 mL) diced celery

2 cups (500 mL) diced onions

½ cup (125 mL) diced leeks

1 cup (250 mL) cooked kidney beans

1 bouquet garni (p. 14)

2 tbsp chopped fresh parsley

salt, to taste

ground black pepper, to taste

1 ½ cup (310 mL) cooked fusilli noodles (optional)

In a medium frying pan on medium-high, heat 1 tbsp oil, and lightly brown venison. Remove meat and deglaze pan with ¼ cup (60 mL) stock. Set aside.

In a large pot on medium heat, sauté vegetables for 3–5 minutes in 1 tbsp oil. Add remainder of stock, kidney beans, and bouquet garni and bring to a boil. Reduce heat and simmer for 45 minutes, until meat is tender. Add parsley and season with salt and pepper. Add cooked pasta, if using. Remove bouquet garni before serving.

MEAT & POULTRY ENTRÉES

PAN-FRIED BUFFALO RIB-EYE STEAKS WITH BLACKBERRY AU JUS

This dish was created to pay homage to pemmican (traditional dried buffalo meat made into a paste with berries and fat), but in a modern version—without the fat—and with a blackberry sauce. It is a great way to enjoy a thick, juicy steak. Serve with sautéed mushrooms and a baked sweet potato or corn on the cob.

Makes 4 servings

2 tbsp canola oil

1 tbsp lemon juice

2 garlic cloves, crushed

salt, to taste

ground black pepper, to taste

4 8-oz (250-g) buffalo rib-eye steaks,
 about 1-in (2.5-cm) thick

¼ cup (60 mL) fresh or frozen blackberries

½ cup (125 mL) dry red wine

1 cup (250 mL) demi-glace (p. 20)

salt, to taste

ground black pepper, to taste

To prepare the marinade: In a small bowl, whisk oil, lemon juice, garlic, salt, and pepper. Place steaks in a glass plate, add marinade, and let sit for a minimum of 1 hour in refrigerator.

In a large frying pan on medium-high heat, panfry steaks 6–8 minutes on each side for rare, 10–12 minutes for medium. Remove steaks, reduce heat to medium, and add berries and red wine. Simmer for 20 minutes until reduced by half. Add demi-glace and bring to boil. Season with salt and pepper, and serve over steaks.

WINE-BRAISED BUFFALO RIBS

The Canadian-born Métis actor and singer Tom Jackson hosted a fundraising dinner for a local food bank in Calgary, Alberta in 2000, which I catered. These ribs are best if reheated the following day for 1 hour at 300°F (150°C). Serve with steamed root vegetables and crusty bread.

◄ **Makes 8 servings** ►

4 lb (1.8 kg) buffalo short ribs

3 tbsp all-purpose flour

1 tsp dry mustard

1 tsp salt

¼–½ tsp ground black pepper

2 tbsp peanut or canola oil

2½–3 cups (626–750 mL) fresh tomato sauce (p.147) or store-bought

¾ cup (185 mL) dry red wine

1½ tbsp prepared yellow mustard

3 tbsp red wine vinegar

Preheat oven to 275°F (140°C).

Trim membrane and fat from meat side of ribs, leaving intact thin connective membrane on bone side. Cut ribs into 3–4-in (8–10-cm) sections. In a large plastic or paper bag, combine flour, dry mustard, salt, and pepper. Add ribs and shake to coat. In a large saucepan on medium-high heat, add oil and ribs and brown on each side. Transfer to a 4–6 qt (3.5–5.5 L) Dutch oven.

In a medium bowl, blend remaining ingredients. Pour over ribs. Cover and bake for 3 hours, until meat is tender.

BRAISED BUFFALO RIBS WITH RED PEPPER PESTO

The Red Pepper Pesto adds depths of sweet-and-sour and bitter flavors to make these some of the most delicious ribs you'll ever taste. Serve with Spring Potatoes with Fireweed Honey Glaze (p. 131), Braised Red Cabbage (p. 127), or Roasted Butternut Squash Ratatouille (p. 130).

◄ **Makes 6 servings** ►

3 lb (1.5 kg) buffalo ribs

freshly cracked black pepper, to taste

2 tbsp canola oil

2 cups (500 mL) diced tomatoes

¼ cup (60 mL) soy sauce

2 tbsp brown sugar

½ cup (125 mL) dark ale (Guinness)

2 tbsp canola oil

6 garlic cloves, crushed

½ cup (125 mL) red pepper pesto (p. 28)

Preheat oven to 325°F (160°C).

Pat buffalo ribs dry with paper towel and season with freshly cracked pepper. In a cast-iron frying pan on medium-high, heat oil, then brown ribs. Place in oven-proof roasting pan.

In a large bowl, combine tomatoes, soy sauce, brown sugar, ale, oil, garlic, and pesto. Pour over ribs and bake, covered, basting every 30 minutes, until meat is tender and begins to fall off the bone when pulled with a fork, about 3 hours.

BUFFALO & CRANBERRY STEW

At the 2010 Winter Olympics, my students and I cooked this stew and served it with bannock during the Métis and Cree events attended by hundreds of people at the First Nations Pavilion. Add Herbed Dumplings (opposite) if desired.

◀ Makes 6–8 servings ▶

2 tbsp canola oil

2 lb (1 kg) buffalo stewing meat, cubed

2½ cups (625 mL) brown stock (p. 16)

1 tsp salt

½ tsp ground black pepper

1 medium onion, chopped

3 garlic cloves, minced

1 cup (250 mL) red wine or 1½ tbsp balsamic vinegar

3 tbsp Worcestershire sauce

1 tbsp paprika

3 whole cloves

2 bay leaves

8 carrots, peeled, split in half lengthwise, and cut in thirds

4 cups (1 L) peeled and cubed potatoes

1¼ cups (310 mL) cranberries, fresh or frozen

3 celery stalks, split in half lengthwise and chopped

4 tbsp maple syrup or 2½ tbsp brown sugar (optional)

½ cup (125 mL) rye or whole wheat flour

In a Dutch oven on medium, heat oil. Add meat and brown on each side. Add stock, salt, and pepper and bring to a boil. Reduce heat to low and simmer, covered, for 30 minutes. Add onions, garlic, wine, Worcestershire sauce, paprika, cloves, and bay leaves. Cover and continue to simmer for 1 hour, stirring every 20 minutes. Add carrots, potatoes, cranberries, and celery. If needed, add enough water to cover vegetables. Stir in maple syrup or brown sugar, especially if vinegar is used. Bring to a boil then reduce heat and simmer. Cover and cook for another 30–45 minutes, or until potatoes are tender. Adjust seasoning to taste, adding more pepper and/or Worcestershire sauce if desired.

In a small bowl, gradually stir 1 cup water into flour. Increase heat so that stew maintains a moderate boil. Add half of flour mixture to stew, stirring continually for 2 minutes, then stir in remainder. Reduce heat to low, add dumplings if desired, and continue to cook.

HERBED DUMPLINGS
Makes about 8 dumplings

2 cups (500 mL) all-purpose flour

4 tsp baking powder

2 tbsp chopped mixed fresh sage, rosemary, wild garlic, and wild onion

½ tsp salt

¾ cup (185 mL) milk

In a large mixing bowl, combine flour, baking powder, herbs, and salt. Add milk, and stir to make a dough. Add more milk or flour to achieve a soft texture. Drop balls of dough, 1 tbsp at a time, into simmering stew. Cover and cook for about 15 minutes without removing lid.

Preheat oven to 400°F (200°C). Bake stew for 50 minutes, until top is browned. Let stand for 20 minutes before serving.

BUFFALO & VEGETABLES BRAISED IN DARK ALE

When I smell this cooking in the oven, it brings back memories of home, where my mother made buffalo stew with bacon and vegetables on a wood stove—although she never used ale, like this recipe does!

◀ **Makes 6–8 servings** ▶

2 lb (1 kg) buffalo (or beef or pork) stewing meat (round, rump, or shoulder), cubed

salt, to taste

ground black pepper, to taste

2 tbsp canola oil

4 strips side bacon, diced

1 large onion, chopped

1 pint dark ale (e.g., Guinness)

1 large orange (zest and juice)

1 garlic clove, minced

2 cups (500 mL) peeled pearl onions (optional)

1 10-oz (300-g) stick unsalted butter

1 tbsp sugar

3 celery stalks, diced

3 large carrots, peeled and chopped

3 large parsnips, peeled and chopped

4 tbsp finely chopped green onions, for garnish

Preheat oven to 300°F (150°C).

Pat cubed meat dry and season with salt and pepper. In a Dutch oven on medium heat, brown meat on each side in oil. Remove meat and transfer to large bowl. Reduce heat and add bacon. Sauté, stirring for 1 minute, then add onions until softened, about 3–5 minutes. Add ale, orange zest and juice, and garlic. Return browned meat to Dutch oven. Cover and cook in oven for 1 ½ hours, stirring every ½ hour.

While stew is cooking, bring a small pot of water to a boil. Add pearl onions and simmer for 3 minutes. Drain onions and rinse under cold water. Peel then set aside. In a small frying pan on medium-high heat, melt butter. Add sugar and onions to pan and sauté for about 8–10 minutes, until lightly caramelized.

Add caramelized pearl onions, celery, carrots, and parsnips to stew. Stir in additional salt and pepper to taste. Return to oven and cook, uncovered, for 1 hour, or until vegetables are soft, stirring every 15–20 minutes. Serve garnished with green onions.

BUFFALO POTATO CASSEROLE

I've prepared this tasty recipe with Métis students to promote their heritage and culture.
Serve with slices of crusty bread to mop up the juices.

◄ **Makes 6–8 servings** ►

2 tbsp butter, for potatoes

2 tbsp canola oil, for potatoes

2½–3 lb (1.25–1.5 kg) potatoes, peeled and sliced
    ¼-in (6-mm) thick

2 medium zucchini, sliced ¼-in (6-mm) thick

½ tsp salt

½ tsp ground black pepper

1 tsp canola oil, for onions

1 large onion, thinly sliced

1 tsp canola oil, for buffalo

1 lb (500 g) ground buffalo

½ cup (125 mL) whole or low-fat milk

1 23-oz (680-mL) can tomato sauce

½ tsp fresh oregano

¼ tsp fresh thyme

½ tsp fresh basil

1 tbsp Worcestershire sauce

2 tbsp butter, for béchamel sauce

¼ cup (60 mL) flour

¾ cup (185 mL) freshly grated aged cheddar cheese

Preheat oven to 375°F (190°C).

In a large saucepan on medium-low heat, melt butter and 2 tbsp oil. Add potatoes and sauté for 6–7 minutes, stirring frequently. Add zucchini, salt, and pepper. Cook for another 5 minutes. Spoon mixture into 13 x 9 x 2 (3.5 L) baking dish and set aside.

In same saucepan on medium, heat 1 tbsp oil. Add onions and sauté until translucent, about 5 minutes. Remove from heat and transfer onions to a bowl. Add 1 tsp more oil to pan, and on medium-high heat, brown ground buffalo. Return cooked onions to pan when buffalo is browned, then stir in milk, tomato sauce, oregano, thyme, basil, and Worcestershire sauce. Combine well. Pour over potato mixture in baking dish.

Clean saucepan and melt 2 tbsp butter on medium heat. Stir in flour and cook for 1 minute. Add milk and stir until mixture boils and thickens slightly. Stir in grated cheese until it melts. Pour over mixture in baking dish and mix well. Bake for 50 minutes, until top is browned. Let stand for 20 minutes before serving.

BROILED BUFFALO PATTIES

This is a great way to enjoy buffalo. Serve these patties on fried bannock (p. 138) with lettuce and tomatoes and your favorite burger condiments.

Makes 6 servings (patties)

2 lb (1 kg) ground buffalo (or beef or venison)

1 onion, diced

1 carrot, finely grated

3 tbsp minced parsley

1 tsp salt

¼ tsp ground black pepper

½ tsp oregano

1 cup (250 mL) breadcrumbs

3 eggs, beaten

1 cup (250 mL) fresh tomato sauce (p. 147) or store-bought

Preheat broiler to medium-high.

In a large bowl, mix all ingredients together. Using an ice cream scoop, form and flatten into patties. Place on baking sheet and broil for about 15 minutes, until internal temperature reaches 170°F (77°C).

SPICY ELK WRAPS

These wraps are healthy and delicious and make a perfect light dinner.

Makes 6 servings

1 tbsp canola oil

1½ lb (750 g) ground elk

4 garlic cloves, minced

1 tbsp minced fresh ginger

¼ cup (60 mL) lime juice

3 tbsp Thai sweet chili sauce

2 tbsp fish sauce

2 tbsp oyster sauce

1 tbsp soy sauce

2 tsp sesame oil

¼ cup (60 mL) chopped fresh cilantro

6 green onions, chopped

2 medium carrots, grated

1 medium head romaine lettuce, core removed, leaves separated

1½ cups (375 mL) crunchy steam-fried noodles, for garnish

1 cup (250 mL) chopped English cucumber, for garnish

In a large frying pan on medium-high, heat oil. Add ground elk and cook for about 10 minutes, stirring occasionally and breaking up any large pieces, until browned. Add garlic and ginger and continue to cook, stirring, for 1 minute until fragrant. Stir in lime juice, sauces, and sesame oil and continue to cook and stir for about 2 minutes. Add cilantro, green onions, and carrots and cook for another 2 minutes.

Fill each lettuce leaf with ½ cup (125 mL) elk mixture. Top with noodles and cucumber.

ELK STEW

This stew, best made the day before serving, reminds me of home on a Sunday afternoon. You can add Herbed Dumplings to make it even more substantial.

◀ **Makes 6 servings** ▶

2 lb (1 kg) elk stew meat (or venison, beef, pork, or veal)

salt, to taste

ground black pepper, to taste

2 tbsp all-purpose flour

2 tbsp canola oil

½ lb (250 g) diced bacon

1 small onion, diced

3 garlic cloves, minced

6 cups game stock (p. 18), brown stock (p. 16), or water

1 28-oz (796-mL) can stewed tomatoes

8 small carrots, diced

2 celery stalks, diced

1 cup (250 mL) fresh wild mushrooms (mixed)

Herbed Dumplings (p.87) (optional)

salt, to taste

ground black pepper, to taste

Season elk with salt and pepper. Dredge in flour and shake off excess. In a heavy pot on medium-high, heat oil. Add bacon and elk and brown on each side. Add onions and sauté until translucent, about 5 minutes. Add garlic, stock, tomatoes, carrots, celery, and mushrooms and bring to a boil. Reduce heat to medium and simmer for 1 hour. Remove from heat and let cool to room temperature. Refrigerate overnight. Reheat before serving and add Herbed Dumplings if desired. Season with salt and pepper.

VENISON ROULADE

A roulade typically consists of a slice of meat rolled around a filling. I use this recipe to show culinary arts students how an ordinary cut of meat can be prepared in a modern and innovative way. Serve with fresh spring salad greens dressed with Lemon Poppyseed Dressing (p. 65) or Balsamic Dressing (p. 64).

◀━━━ **Makes 4 servings** ▶━━

1 lb (500 g) inside or top round venison or beef

1 medium onion, roughly chopped

5 whole fresh garlic cloves

3 slices fresh bread, crusts removed, torn into pieces

¼ cup (60 mL) Dijon mustard

1 tbsp Worcestershire sauce

salt, to taste

ground black pepper, to taste

1½ cups (375 mL) sage hazelnut pesto (p. 27)

1 tbsp canola oil

Preheat oven to 200°F (95°C).

Pound venison or beef with meat mallet until ½-in (1-cm) thick.

In a food processor, purée onions, garlic, bread, mustard, and Worcestershire sauce to paste consistency. Place venison on length of plastic wrap and season with salt and pepper. Spread purée evenly across meat. Rub with pesto. Roll up tightly, and tie with butcher twine.

In a frying pan on high heat, sear roulade on each side in canola oil. (Don't cook through; just brown the meat) Let cool, then seal tightly in plastic wrap, and wrap in foil.

Place roulade in roasting pan. Add water to pan until roulade is ¾ immersed. Bake roulade until it reaches internal temperature of 140°F (60°C), about 45 minutes. Let rest for 10 minutes before serving.

VENISON STIR-FRY WITH FRESH GARDEN VEGETABLES

A fusion between East and West, this is a simple-to-prepare yet healthy meal. Serve over rice or noodles.

◄──── **Makes 4–6 servings** ►────►

1 lb (500 g) boneless venison, sliced into ¾-in
    (2-cm) strips

2 tbsp soy sauce

2 garlic cloves, minced

2 tsp minced fresh ginger

1 tbsp sesame oil

1 each red, green, and yellow bell peppers,
    seeded and thinly sliced

1 small zucchini, sliced diagonally

1 carrot, sliced diagonally

⅛ cup (30 mL) light soy sauce

½ cup (125 mL) demi-glace (p. 20)

In a large glass baking dish or bowl, marinate venison strips in soy sauce, garlic, and ginger for 2–4 hours in the refrigerator.

In a frying pan on high, heat oil to smoking point, and quickly sauté venison, about 3–4 minutes. Remove from pan. Add vegetables to pan and sauté for 2 minutes. Add soy sauce and demi-glace, and bring to a simmer for about 4 minutes. Return venison to pan and mix thoroughly.

VENISON TOURTIÈRE

A traditional French-Canadian Christmas or New Year's Eve holiday meal, tourtière is usually made with finely diced pork or veal. My version uses venison, but you can also use buffalo. The bacon is traditional and gives it a great smoky flavor, but using canola oil to brown the meat is a healthier option.

◀━━━ **Makes 6 servings** ━▶━

3 slices chopped bacon or 2 tbsp canola oil

1 lb (500 g) minced lean venison or buffalo

¼ cup (60 mL) chopped onions

¼ tsp ground cloves

½ tsp salt

¼ tsp dried savory

¼ tsp ground black pepper

1 bay leaf

pastry for 9-in (23-cm) two-crust pie

Preheat oven to 425°F (220°C).

In a large pot on medium heat, cook bacon (or heat oil, if using). Stir in meat, onions, cloves, salt, savory, and pepper. Add bay leaf and ½ cup (125 mL) water. Simmer uncovered, for about 20 minutes, stirring occasionally. Remove bay leaf, let cool, and skim off fat. Fill pastry crust in pie plate with meat mixture. Cover with pastry, seal edges, and cut small steam vents in top of crust. Bake for about 30 minutes, until lightly browned.

PAN-FRIED CARIBOU STEAKS WITH GREEN PEPPERCORN SAUCE

A steak preparation incorporating caribou, which is lighter tasting than most game meats. Green peppercorns are the unripe seeds of **Piper nigrum.** *Serve with Wild Rice Pilaf (p. 134) and steamed wild greens.*

◀ **Makes 4 servings** ▶

¼ cup (60 mL) canola oil

8 medallions of caribou (or beef, veal, or venison)

1 tbsp chopped shallots

¼ cup (60 mL) red wine

1 tbsp whole green peppercorns in brine

1 cup (250 mL) demi-glace (p. 20)

1 tbsp 35% cream

salt, to taste

ground black pepper, to taste

In a large frying pan on medium-high, heat oil. Add caribou and sear for about 2 minutes per side. Remove from pan and set aside on serving platter. Drain excess fat from pan and return to heat. Add shallots and sauté for about 2 minutes. Add red wine and simmer until reduced by half. Add peppercorns and demi-glace and bring to a simmer for 3–4 minutes. Stir in cream, and season with salt and pepper. Pour sauce over caribou.

THREE-GAME MEATBALLS

The flavors of wild boar, venison, and buffalo in this recipe complement the fresh herbs and cheese beautifully. Serve these with Fresh Tomato Sauce (p. 147) and Homemade Pasta (p. 143), or as an appetizer with a Wild Berry Sauce (p. 175).

Makes 4–6 servings

½ lb (250 g) ground buffalo

½ lb (250 g) ground venison (or beef)

½ lb (250 g) ground wild boar (or pork)

1 cup (250 mL) diced onions

4 garlic cloves, minced

2 tbsp Worcestershire sauce

1 egg, beaten

1 cup (250 mL) breadcrumbs

1 tbsp chopped fresh Italian parsley

1 tbsp chopped fresh thyme

1 tbsp chopped fresh basil

½ cup (125 mL) freshly grated Parmesan cheese

Preheat oven to 375°F (175°C).

In a large bowl, combine all ingredients and mix thoroughly. Roll into 2-in (5-cm) balls. Place meatballs in lightly oiled large baking dish and bake for 45 minutes.

CRANBERRY SWEET & SOUR GOOSE BREAST

I tried this recipe for the first time in Northern Quebec, along the shores of James Bay, and loved the combination of ingredients.

◄ **Makes 4 servings** ►

4 large boneless goose breasts

2 tbsp salt

1 tsp ground black pepper

2 tbsp sugar

6 medium onions, thinly sliced

2 tbsp olive oil

½ cup (125 mL) sherry vinegar

½ cup (125 mL) honey

1 cup (250 mL) fresh cranberries

In a large baking dish, rub goose breasts with salt, pepper, and sugar. Let stand at room temperature for 3–5 hours or overnight in refrigerator. Rinse salt, pepper, and sugar from goose.

Preheat broiler to high. Broil 5–6 minutes per side. Remove and set aside.

In a large frying pan on medium heat, sauté onions in oil until translucent, about 5 minutes. Add vinegar and honey, and simmer for 3–4 minutes. Stir in fresh cranberries and pour over goose.

TOODY NI JUNIPER DUCK

This recipe quickly becomes a favorite of anyone I prepare it for. While it's quite simple to make, the end product is spectacular. I like to serve it with Roasted Yams and Beets (p. 129) or over steamed fiddleheads when in season.

◀■ **Makes 2 servings** ▶

2 6-oz (175-g) boneless duck breasts

salt, to taste

ground black pepper, to taste

1 large shallot, chopped

1 tbsp crushed juniper berries

2 tsp canola oil

1 tbsp juniper gin

⅓ cup (80 mL) red wine

½ cup (125 mL) duck or chicken stock (p. 15) or demi-glace (p.20)

1 tbsp chopped fresh sage

Preheat broiler to high.

Season duck with salt and pepper and place, skin side up, on a rack in a broiling pan.

In a small saucepan on medium-high heat, sauté shallots and juniper berries in oil. Deglaze pan with gin and red wine. Add stock and simmer for about 20 minutes, until liquid is reduced by half. Pour sauce over duck and broil for 5 minutes. Reduce oven temperature to 375°F (190°C) and baste duck with sauce. Roast for 10 minutes, until duck is cooked to medium rare. Arrange on 2 plates and spoon sauce over duck.

RABBIT FRICASSEE

When I was a kid, our mother would often have a version of this recipe and her homemade bread ready for us for supper. Whether you use rabbit or chicken, this is real comfort food.

◀ **Makes 4 servings** ▶

1 rabbit (or 1 whole chicken), cut into serving pieces

3 tbsp all-purpose flour, seasoned with salt and pepper

½ cup (125 mL) butter

2 tbsp olive oil

3 bacon slices, chopped

1 cup (250 mL) finely chopped onions

2 cups (500 mL) quartered button mushrooms

1 tbsp chopped garlic

½ cup (125 mL) white wine

2 cups (500 mL) chicken stock (p. 15) or water

2 medium Yukon Gold potatoes, chopped

½ tsp chopped dried thyme

½ tsp chopped dried sage

½ tsp chopped dried rosemary

salt, to taste

ground black pepper, to taste

1 bay leaf

Herbed Dumplings (p. 87) (optional)

½ cup (125 mL) 35% cream (or evaporated milk) (optional)

1 tbsp chopped fresh parsley, for garnish

Dredge rabbit in seasoned flour and shake off excess. In a Dutch oven or large cast-iron pan on medium, heat butter and olive oil. Add rabbit and bacon and cook until rabbit is golden brown. Drain fat from pan and add onions, mushrooms, and garlic. Cook for 5 minutes, until onions are translucent. Deglaze pan with white wine. Add stock. Bring to a low boil then reduce heat and simmer for 45 minutes. Add potatoes, thyme, sage, rosemary, salt, pepper, and bay leaf. Simmer for 30 minutes, until rabbit is tender.

If desired, add Herbed Dumplings after 10 minutes, and continue to cook for remaining 20 minutes with pot covered. Remove rabbit from pan and place onto platter to keep warm. Remove bay leaf from sauce. If using cream, stir into sauce. Bring to a boil, then reduce to medium heat. Simmer for about 20 minutes, until sauce is reduced by half. Pour sauce over rabbit and sprinkle with minced parsley.

RASPBERRY-GLAZED RABBIT ROULADE

The Sage Hazelnut Pesto takes this roulade to new heights of flavor.

◀━━━ **Makes about 1 cup (250 mL)** ━━━▶

RABBIT ROULADE

6 boneless rabbit legs (or chicken)

2 tbsp each chopped fresh sage, thyme, and oregano

salt, to taste

ground black pepper, to taste

½ cup (125 mL) sage hazelnut pesto (p. 27)

2 cups (500 mL) baby dandelion greens or baby arugula

3 tbsp olive oil

RASPBERRY GLAZE

1 cup (250 mL) sugar

1 cup (250 mL) raspberry vinegar

2 tbsp raspberry preserves or jam

½ cup (125 mL) fresh raspberries

Preheat oven to 350°F (180°C).

Place rabbit legs into an oiled plastic bag, and pound to a ¼-in (6-mm) thickness with a mallet. Remove legs from bag. Season with fresh herbs, salt, and pepper. Spread pesto evenly across each leg. In a pot fitted with a steamer, steam dandelion greens until slightly wilted but still green. Spread greens over pesto. Roll up tightly and tie with butcher twine.

In a large cast-iron pan on medium, heat oil. Brown rabbit on each side, until golden. Bake for 20 minutes. Remove from oven and let rest for 5 minutes before slicing.

For the glaze:
In a large saucepan, bring sugar and raspberry vinegar to a boil. Reduce heat and simmer until reduced by half. Add raspberry preserves and fresh raspberries and let simmer for another 1–2 minutes. Pour over slices of roulate before serving.

FISH & SEAFOOD ENTRÉES

SEARED NORTH PACIFIC TUNA WITH BEETS, DANDELION GREENS & HORSERADISH CREAM

My students and I cooked this at the Canadian Culinary Federation Conference in Vancouver in 2011. The horseradish has a bit of a bite, offset by the cream—perfect with tender tuna and steamed greens topped with Lemon Poppy Seed Dressing.

◀ **Makes 4 servings** ▶

8 baby red or striped beets

8 baby golden beets

salt, to taste

ground black pepper, to taste

2 tbsp olive oil

1 cup (250 mL) cider vinegar

4 tbsp sugar

4 6-oz (175-g) fresh Pacific tuna fillets (skin on)

1 tsp chopped roasted garlic (p. 38)

1 tsp lemon juice

1 tsp chopped fresh thyme

1 tsp chopped fresh dill

1 large bunch dandelion greens, stems trimmed

2 tbsp lemon poppy seed dressing (p. 65)

¼ cup (60 mL) horseradish cream (opposite)

Preheat oven to 350°F (180°C). Cover baking tray with sheet of aluminum foil. Trim and wash beets then season with salt, pepper, and olive oil. Roast for 30 minutes, until tender (if pierced with a paring knife, beet should slide off knife easily). Peel by hand while still warm; skin should slide off. In a medium bowl, combine cider vinegar and sugar. Marinate beets in mixture until ready to serve.

Rub tuna fillets with roasted garlic and lemon juice and season with thyme and dill. In an oiled, pre-heated cast-iron frying pan on high, sear fillets for about 1 minute per side.

In a pot fitted with a steamer, steam dandelion greens until slightly wilted but still green. Arrange greens on 4 plates. Top with sliced beets and lemon poppy seed dressing. Place tuna on plates and drizzle with horseradish cream.

HORSERADISH CREAM
Makes 1 cup (250 ml)

1 cup (250 mL) shredded fresh
   horseradish root
½ cup (125 mL) fish velouté (p. 23)
1 tbsp dill pesto (p. 26)
2 tbsp white wine
1 tbsp chopped shallots
2 tbsp cream
salt, to taste
ground black pepper, to taste

In a medium saucepan on high heat, bring all ingredients except cream, salt, and pepper to a boil, then reduce to low. Simmer until sauce is reduced in volume by half. Add cream and, continuing to simmer on low, reduce by half again. Season with salt and pepper.

BRAISED PACIFIC HALIBUT

Pacific halibut are among the largest fish native to the northern fishing waters, and among the tastiest. Serve with Wilted Stinging Nettles (p. 124) and Spring Potatoes with Fireweed Honey Glaze (p. 131).

Makes 4 servings

4 6-oz (175-g) halibut fillets

3 tbsp all-purpose flour

salt, to taste, for flour

ground black pepper, to taste, for flour

2 tbsp canola oil or butter

2 tbsp minced shallots

2 tbsp minced garlic

½ cup (125 mL) dry white wine

½ cup (125 mL) fish stock (p. 14)

salt, to taste

ground black pepper, to taste

Dredge halibut fillets in flour seasoned with salt and pepper and shake off excess. In a large frying pan on medium, heat oil or butter. Cook seasoned fish skin side up for 6–7 minutes, depending on thickness. Flip, and cook for 4 more minutes. Stir in shallots and garlic and sauté for 1 minute. Add white wine and stock. Cover and cook for another 4 minutes. Season with salt and pepper.

PAN-SEARED HALIBUT CHEEKS WITH SEAWEED

This is one of my favorite dishes when halibut is in season. The halibut cheeks are delicate and flavorful; when seared with seaweed, they taste amazing. Serve with Wild Rice Pilaf (p. 134) and Roasted Yams and Beets (p. 129), and top with Butter Sauce (below).

◀ **Makes 4 servings** ▶

12 ¼-lb (125-g) fresh halibut cheeks

¾ cup (185 mL) all-purpose flour

1 tsp salt

1 tsp ground white pepper

2 tbsp finely chopped nori (seaweed)

4 tbsp canola oil

BUTTER SAUCE
Makes 1 cup (250 ml)

1 tbsp minced shallots

2 tbsp lemon juice

2 tbsp white wine

8 tbsp unsalted butter, cubed

1 tbsp minced fresh chives

1 tbsp finely chopped nori (seaweed)

sea salt, to taste

ground white pepper, to taste

Rinse halibut cheeks and pat dry. In a large bowl, combine flour, salt, pepper, and nori. Dredge halibut in flour mixture and shake off excess. In a large frying pan on medium, heat oil. Sauté halibut cheeks 1–2 minutes per side.

For the sauce:
In a small saucepan on medium heat, bring shallots, lemon juice, and white wine to a simmer until liquid is reduced by half. Reduce heat to low. Whisk in butter cubes one at a time until sauce starts to emulsify (thicken). Add chives and nori. Season with salt and pepper. Pour over halibut cheeks before serving.

POACHED SALMON

This recipe is the basis for Niçoise Salad (p. 58), Salmon Cakes (p. 116), Poached Salmon Supreme (p. 118), West Coast Seafood Rolls (p. 119), and more.

Makes 4 servings

4 6-oz (175 g) Pacific wild salmon fillets

4 cups (1 L) court bouillon (p. 22)

In a large stock pot on medium-high heat, simmer salmon in bouillon until tender, 5–8 minutes per lb (500 g), 10–15 minutes total. Remove to cool and use in any number of recipes, including those listed above.

GRILLED PACIFIC SALMON WITH FRESH HERBS

The fresh herbs add great flavor to the salmon. Serve this on baked bannock (p. 138) as you would a hamburger, topped with your favorite condiments.

◀ Makes 4 servings ▶

4 4-oz (115-g) fresh Pacific salmon fillets

¼ tsp fresh lemon juice

½ tsp each finely chopped fresh dill, thyme, and parsley

salt, to taste

ground black pepper, to taste

2 tbsp canola oil, for salmon

Oil barbecue and preheat to 375°F (190°C). Season salmon with fresh lemon juice, herbs, salt, and pepper and lightly brush with oil. Lay fillet skin side up and at an angle on barbecue for 3½ minutes. Angle in opposite direction to make a crosshatch and grill for another 3½ minutes. Flip salmon and cook for 6–7 minutes.

SALMON CAKES WITH WILTED GREENS

My mother used to make salmon cakes from scratch for our father, who loved these. You don't have to use poached salmon, as canned or leftover baked salmon works just as well. Freshly grated horseradish mixed into the salmon adds loft and texture to the cakes, as well as imparting its inimitable flavor, in subdued form, to the whole. Serve with Horseradish Cream (p. 109). This one's for you, Mom and Dad!

◀ Makes 12 cakes ▶

4 cups (1 L) flaked poached salmon (p. 113)

3 tbsp grated onions

½ cup (125 mL) freshly grated horseradish

2 tbsp Dijon mustard

½ cup (125 mL) chopped flat-leaf parsley

2 eggs, beaten

½ tsp salt

2 tsp ground black pepper

3 tbsp canola oil (1½ tbsp for cooking first batch of cakes, and 1½ tbsp for second)

3 tbsp butter (1½ tbsp for cooking first batch of cakes, and 1½ tbsp for second)

1½ cups (375 mL) fine fresh breadcrumbs, seasoned with a little salt and pepper

1 tbsp butter, for greens

6 cups (1.5 L) baby spinach leaves, Asian mustard greens, or a mix of baby kale and red and green chard

salt, to taste

juice of 2 lemons

Preheat oven to 300°F (150°C).

In a large bowl, combine salmon, onions, horseradish, mustard, parsley, eggs, salt, and pepper. Mash all ingredients until well mixed. Form into 12 balls, each about the size of a small lemon. Flatten into cakes and set aside in a single layer on aluminum foil or waxed paper.

In a skillet large enough to hold half the cakes at once, on medium, heat 1½ tbsp of oil and 1½ tbsp of butter. Sprinkle half the breadcrumbs onto sheet of foil or waxed paper. Press 6 cakes into crumbs, coating both sides. Place cakes into skillet and cook for about 2 minutes on each side, until crispy brown. Remove and set aside to drain on paper towels, then place in oven to keep warm. Add remaining oil and butter to skillet. Coat remaining cakes with crumbs, then cook for 2 minutes per side. Drain on paper towels and keep warm in oven.

In a large skillet on medium heat, melt remaining 1 tbsp butter. Add greens, cover, and cook for 30–40 seconds. Uncover, stir, re-cover, and cook until greens have just wilted but still retain their color, another 30 seconds. Sprinkle with salt. Increase heat to high, and pour in lemon juice. Stir and cook for another 15–20 seconds.

To serve, arrange bed of wilted greens on platter or individual plates and top with salmon cakes.

POACHED SALMON SUPREME WITH WHITE WINE SAUCE & JULIENNED VEGETABLES

I love to see my students' faces when they try this method of preparing salmon for the first time. The fish gets wonderful flavor from the poaching liquid, and the flesh is moist and flaky.

Makes 4 servings

4 4–6 oz (115–175 g) boneless wild Pacific salmon fillets, skin removed

2 carrots, peeled and julienned

2 leeks, white part only, julienned

1 small onion, julienned

¼ cup (60 mL) white wine

¼ cup (60 mL) white wine sauce (below)

1 tbsp fish velouté (p. 23)

WHITE WINE SAUCE
Makes ½ cup (125 ml)

¼ cup (60 mL) fish stock (p. 14)

2 tbsp white wine

¼ cup (60 mL) minced shallots

¼ cup (60 mL) whole or low-fat milk

2 tbsp fish velouté (p. 23)

Poach salmon following the recipe on p. 113. Let salmon rest for 2–3 minutes.

In a small saucepan on medium heat, simmer julienned vegetables and white wine for 3–4 minutes. Add white wine sauce and finish by adding fish velouté. Pour sauce and vegetables over poached salmon.

For the sauce:
In a large pot on high heat, bring stock, white wine, and shallots to a boil. Reduce heat to low and simmer about 5 minutes. Add milk and continue to simmer until reduced by half. Add fish velouté and cook for an additional 5 minutes. Strain through a fine sieve.

WEST COAST SEAFOOD BOIL

This dish reflects how Aboriginal people traditionally ate their seafood on beaches all up and down the West Coast. This modern version, however, has a little bite. Serve with drawn butter on the side (see below).

Makes 4 servings

2 whole Dungeness crab

8 Pacific prawns

¼ cup (60 mL) butter

2 medium onions, diced

4 garlic cloves, minced

½ tsp cayenne pepper

½ tsp garlic powder

½ tsp onion powder

½ tsp paprika

½ tsp white pepper

16 medium-sized Manila clams

1 cup (250 mL) white wine

2 blanched and halved corn cobs

8 baby Yukon gold potatoes, blanched

2 cooked smoked chorizo or hot Italian sausages, chopped

6 large scallops

In a large pot on high, bring salted water to a rapid boil. Add crab and cook, 7–8 minutes per pound. Drain and clean, cut into quarters, and set aside. Clean and devein prawns. Set aside.

In the same large pot on medium heat, add butter and onions. Sauté for 2 minutes. Add garlic, cayenne, garlic and onion powder, paprika, and white pepper and sauté for an additional minute. Add clams and white wine. Cover and allow to steam for 3–4 minutes, or until clams open. Add prawns, corn, potatoes, sausages, scallops, and crab and simmer for 4–6 minutes.

**DRAWN
(CLARIFIED) BUTTER**
½ cup (125 mL) unsalted butter

In a small saucepan on medium heat, melt butter. Bring to a boil. When milk solids have separated and sunk to bottom of pan, remove from heat and ladle out clarified butter. Keep warm until ready to serve.

WEST COAST SEAFOOD ROLLS

I developed this East-West fusion recipe with a class of culinary students in Montreal in the mid-1990s, and since then I've served it at banquets in several other cities in Europe. A bamboo sushi mat, available in most gourmet or Asian cookware shops, will help you roll the sushi. Slice each roll into 8 pieces and serve with Horseradish Cream (p. 109).

◀ Makes 4 servings ▶

HALIBUT MOUSSE

1 lb (500 g) halibut, cod, flounder, or sea bass, chopped into 1-in (2.5-cm) pieces

1½ tsp salt

cayenne pepper, to taste

3 egg whites

1½ cups (375 mL) whipping cream

1 tbsp grated onions

1 tsp fresh lemon juice

½ cup (125 mL) chopped fresh dill

salt, to taste

ground black pepper, to taste

In a food processor, purée halibut until it forms a ball on the blade. Stop food processor, scrape down sides, and add salt, cayenne, egg whites, and cream. Pulse until mousse is just blended, but do not over-beat. Transfer by large spoonfuls to a sieve. With back of rubber spatula or serving spoon, force mixture through sieve into bowl. By hand, stir in onions, lemon juice, and dill. Season to taste with salt and pepper, and chill in refrigerator for 2 hours.

SEAFOOD ROLLS

4 nori sheets (Japanese sushi seaweed)

1 lb (500 g) thinly sliced cold smoked wild Pacific sockeye salmon

½ lb (250 g) cubed poached wild Pacific sockeye salmon (p. 113)

½ lb (250 g) cleaned, steamed, and shucked fresh clams

½ lb (250 g) chopped poached prawns

½ lb (250 g) cleaned, steamed, and shucked fresh mussels

4 cups (1 L) court bouillon (p. 22)

Place sheet of plastic wrap over bamboo sushi mat. Lay one sheet of seaweed on top. Place slices of smoked salmon over seaweed sheet, laying them side by side until sheet is covered. Mix remainder of seafood into halibut mixture and spoon ½ cup (125 mL) evenly across middle of sheet. Roll nori with the mat and seal tightly with plastic wrap. Repeat 3 more times. Wrap rolls with foil over plastic wrap and let chill in refrigerator for 1 hour.

Preheat oven to 300°F (150°C).

In a large pot on high, bring court bouillon
to a boil. Place rolls in a large baking
dish. Pour hot bouillon into baking dish
half-way up sides. Bake for 40 minutes,
until rolls feel firm to touch. Remove rolls
from baking dish. Peel off foil, and leave in
plastic wrap. Chill in refrigerator for up to 4
hours. Slice before serving.

VEGETARIAN ENTRÉES & SIDE DISHES

WILTED STINGING NETTLES

If you're going into the wild to collect stinging nettles, be sure to wear gloves—contact with the little spikes on the leaves and stems of these plants will make your skin sting and break out in a rash. Once cooked, however, they not only become harmless but tender and delicious and full of nutrients.
Serve with Braised Pacific Halibut (p. 110).

Makes 4 servings

8 cups (2 L) fresh nettles, stems removed
   (use gloves)

2 tbsp olive oil

2 tbsp minced shallots

2 tbsp minced garlic

½ cup (125 mL) dry white wine

½ cup (125 mL) fish stock (p. 14)

salt, to taste

ground black pepper, to taste

In a large pot on high heat, blanch nettles in boiling salted water for 10 seconds, then remove and immerse in an ice-water bath. This will ensure nettles are soft yet retain their color.

In a large pan on medium, heat oil. Add shallots, garlic, and nettles, and sauté for 1 minute. Add wine and stock. Cover and cook for 4 more minutes. Season to taste with salt and pepper.

CURRIED DANDELION GREENS WITH GOLDEN ONIONS & CASHEWS

Serve this as a side dish for a game steak or as a main topped with seafood, such as seared salmon or halibut.

Makes 4 servings

1 large onion, cut lengthwise into ¼-in (6-mm) wedges

3 tbsp olive oil, for onions

salt, to taste

½ cup (125 mL) coarsely chopped, salted and roasted cashews

2 tsp curry powder

1 tsp ground coriander

1 tsp ground cumin

½ tsp ground cinnamon

1 tsp mustard seeds

¼ tsp cayenne pepper

3 tbsp olive oil, for greens

1 lb (500 g) spinach, tough stems discarded

1 lb (500 g) Swiss chard, center stems discarded

1 lb (500 g) dandelion greens, tough stems discarded

In a heavy 10-in (25-cm) frying pan on medium heat, sauté onions in oil, stirring occasionally, until deep golden brown, 15–20 minutes. Season with salt. Add cashews and continue to cook, stirring occasionally, until nuts are a shade darker, about 3 minutes.

In a bowl, combine all spices. Stir 1½ tsp spice mix into onions and cashews and cook, stirring until fragrant, about 30 seconds. Remove from heat.

In a heavy pot on medium-high heat, heat 3 tbsp oil until hot but not smoking. Add remaining spice mix, stirring until fragrant, about 30 seconds. Immediately stir in spinach, chard, dandelion greens, and ½ cup (125 mL) water. Cook, stirring occasionally, until most of the liquid has evaporated and greens are tender, about 4–6 minutes. Serve greens sprinkled with onion and cashew mixture.

BRAISED RED CABBAGE

We grew up eating fried cabbage with bacon—which was pretty good—but I like the flavor of this braised recipe, which is a natural fit for game meats.

◀ Makes 4–6 servings ▶

1 red cabbage

¼ cup (60 mL) canola oil

1 onion, diced

2 tbsp balsamic vinegar

1 apple, diced

2 tbsp brown sugar

2 cups (500 mL) apple juice

Cut cabbage in quarters and remove core. Slice cabbage into thin strips. In a large saucepan on medium, heat oil and sauté onions until translucent, about 5 minutes. Add cabbage and continue to sauté for about 10 minutes. Add remaining ingredients and bring to boil. Reduce heat to low, cover pan, and simmer for 40 minutes.

ROASTED YAMS & BEETS

Serve as a side with Toody Ni Juniper Duck (p. 100) or any of the salmon dishes in this book.
This recipe can be served warm or cold.

◄ Makes 4–6 servings ►

8 baby red or striped beets

8 baby golden beets

3 tbsp olive oil

1 tbsp coarse salt

½ tsp ground black pepper

1 tsp ground cinnamon

1 tsp brown sugar

1 tsp ground cumin

1 tsp honey

2 medium yams, peeled and cubed

1 cup (250 mL) cider vinegar

4 tbsp sugar

salt, to taste

ground white pepper, to taste

Preheat oven to 375°F (190°C).

Scrub beets well to clean and trim ends. Place on foil wrap and drizzle with oil, salt, and pepper. Wrap foil around beets and set aside. In a small bowl, combine cinnamon, brown sugar, cumin, and honey and toss with cubed yams to coat well. Wrap in foil. Bake both foil wraps for 30 minutes. Remove yams and beets from foil and let cool. Peel beets by hand; skins should slide right off. Slice beets thinly across the grain. In a bowl, toss beets and yams with cider vinegar and sugar. Season to taste with salt and white pepper.

ROASTED BUTTERNUT SQUASH RATATOUILLE

When I first introduced this recipe to my students, it raised a few eyebrows, but it introduced them to a whole new world of flavors.

Makes 4–6 servings

1 medium butternut squash, peeled and halved, fibers scooped out, and cubed (¾ in [2 cm])

salt, to taste

ground black pepper, to taste

¼ cup (60 mL) honey

2 tsp canola oil, for squash

1 tsp canola oil, for sautéing

1 cup (250 mL) peeled and diced carrots

1 cup (250 mL) cleaned and diced leeks, white part only

1 cup (250 mL) diced zucchini

1 cup (250 mL) diced Granny Smith apple

½ cup (125 mL) minced shallots

1 cup (250 mL) vegetable stock or chicken stock (p. 15)

Preheat oven to 375°F (190°C).

Season squash with salt and pepper, and drizzle with honey. Place in a roasting pan and toss with 2 tsp oil. Roast until tender, tossing occasionally, for about 25 minutes.

In a large, non-stick frying pan, heat 1 tsp oil. Add roasted squash and diced carrots, and sauté for 3 minutes. Add leeks and sauté for 2 minutes. Add zucchini, apples, and shallots, and cook for 3 more minutes. Stir in broth and season with additional salt and pepper if desired. Simmer until vegetables are tender but not too soft, about 15 minutes. Serve warm.

SPRING POTATOES WITH FIREWEED HONEY GLAZE

The sweet glaze in this recipe takes spring potatoes to new heights. Fireweed honey is produced in western Canada and northwestern US; if not available, regular honey will suffice.

◄ Makes 4 servings ►

12 fingerling potatoes

1 tsp unsalted butter

1 tsp chopped fresh parsley

2 tbsp fireweed honey

salt, to taste

ground black pepper, to taste

In a large saucepan on high, boil potatoes with enough water to cover for 15–20 minutes, or until tender but still firm. Drain potatoes and toss gently with butter, parsley, honey, salt, and pepper.

GRILLED VEGETABLE TERRINE

I've served this elegant vegetarian dish (prepared in a terrine, an earthenware vessel) at a number of banquets. If you don't own a terrine, you can use a loaf pan. The dish is served cold, and the loaf is sliced, like a pâté. Make it at least a day before serving, as it needs to set overnight.

◀ **Makes 6–8 servings** ▶

VEGETABLES

4 tbsp olive oil

4 red bell peppers, seeded and quartered

4 yellow bell peppers, seeded and quartered

4 Japanese eggplants

4 zucchini

2 leeks, split lengthwise and cleaned

3 portobello mushrooms, stemmed

2 tbsp olive oil

salt, to taste

ground black pepper, to taste

½ cup (125 mL) sliced green beans

TERRINE

⅓ cup (80 mL) softened cream cheese

2 eggs

2¼ tsp salt

1 tsp white pepper

1 envelope powdered gelatin

Preheat broiler to high.

Brush 2 tbsp oil on bell peppers laid on a cookie sheet. Broil until skins blister and char, turning occasionally to blacken all sides. Transfer to a bowl and cover with a plate. Let cool. Remove skin from peppers, then cut into ¾-in (2-cm) strips. Set aside.

Using a mandoline if you have one, or a sharp knife, slice eggplants, zucchini, leeks, and mushrooms lengthwise into ⅛-in (3-mm) strips. Brush strips with 2 tbsp oil and season with salt and pepper.

In a large frying pan on high heat, sauté eggplants and zucchini 1–2 minutes per side. Remove, and set aside. Repeat process with leeks and portobello mushrooms.

In a medium pot, bring salted water to a rapid boil. Add green beans and cook for about 4 minutes, until tender but still bright green. Drop beans into ice-water bath for 5 minutes, remove, and pat dry. Set aside.

For the terrine:
Preheat oven to 400°F (200°C).

Line terrine pan or 9 x 5-in (2-L) loaf pan with plastic wrap, leaving enough hanging over edges to cover contents when filled.

In an electric mixer bowl with paddle attachment, beat cream cheese at medium speed until smooth. Beat in eggs, salt, and pepper.

Brush bottom of terrine pan with a little cream cheese mixture. Layer half of each ingredient, in this order: bell peppers, eggplants, green beans, leeks, zucchini, and mushrooms. Spread half of cream cheese mixture on vegetables and sprinkle with gelatin. Repeat with remainder of vegetables and cream cheese, saving some bell peppers for garnishing top of terrine. Fold plastic wrap over top and tightly cover with double layer of foil. Place terrine in a baking pan and add boiling water until pan is 2/3 full. Bake for 75 minutes or until internal temperature reaches 185°F (85°C).

Remove terrine from baking pan and let cool. Cover terrine with cardboard cut to fit and place weight on top of terrine. (*Note:* Clean, foil-wrapped bricks work well, as do large cans of vegetables.) Refrigerate overnight (8 hours).

Remove weight, unwrap terrine, and carefully invert onto plate. Cover and refrigerate unless serving immediately. Terrine will keep in refrigerator for up to 4 days.

WILD RICE PILAF

The flavor of wild rice is complemented well by wild mushrooms. Stock made from game, such as venison, adds just the right flavor, but you can substitute beef or vegetable stock and the pilaf will still be delicious.

◄ Makes 4 servings ►

1 tbsp canola oil

1 cup (250 mL) diced onions

1 cup (250 mL) diced celery

2 tsp chopped fresh garlic

1 cup (250 mL) chopped chanterelle or
   morel mushrooms

1½ cups (375 mL) long-grained wild rice

3 cups (750 mL) game stock (p. 18) or beef stock

½ tsp chopped fresh thyme

¼ tsp salt

½ cup (125 mL) diced red bell peppers

In a heavy pot on medium, heat oil. Sauté onions and celery until translucent, about 5 minutes. Add garlic and mushrooms, and cook for 5 more minutes. Add rice and stir, allowing rice to slightly brown. Add stock, thyme, and salt. Bring to a boil. Cover and let simmer for 45 minutes, until rice is cooked and most of the liquid absorbed. Stir in bell peppers.

Mahekun **WILD RICE CASSEROLE**

Co-author Robert Gairns contributed this recipe to the original **Feast for All Seasons** *book.*
He told me stories about his numerous hunting trips to northern Ontario, where he would serve this
dish with deer. **Mahekun** *is the Plains Cree word for wolf. A Métis actor friend of Robert's, Harry Daniels,*
tagged him with the name years ago. This casserole is excellent as a stuffing or a side dish.
Serve with baked or fried bannock (p. 138). Thanks, Robert!

Makes 4–6 servings

½ lb (250 g) *man-o-min* (Native-supplied wild rice)

½ tsp sea salt

1 tbsp unsalted butter

1 large onion, diced

1 garlic clove, minced

1 large apple, peeled and diced

½ lb (250 g) chopped wild shiitake or
white mushrooms

½ tsp ground black pepper

juice of 1 orange

¼ cup (60 mL) dry vermouth

¼ cup (60 mL) cognac or brandy

Wash rice thoroughly and drain well. Place in bottom of large, deep pot. Place your hand flat over rice and add enough water to just cover your hand. Add salt. Cover pot and bring water to a boil. Cook for 30 minutes, making sure water does not burn off, until rice is tender and liquid is absorbed. Transfer rice to a bowl to cool.

In a large frying pan on medium-high heat, melt butter. Sauté onions until translucent, about 5 minutes. Add garlic and sauté for 1 minute. Add apple and sauté for 2–3 minutes. Add mushrooms and pepper and sauté another 2 minutes. Stir in orange juice and vermouth and simmer for 5 minutes. Add cognac and carefully light with a long fire-place match. When flame burns out, stir in rice, and cook for 2 minutes, until rice is heated through.

CORN FRITTERS

A tasty change from clam or apple fritters. To make it even healthier, instead of a deep fryer you can cook these in a cast-iron pan with minimal oil, like a pancake, to achieve the same texture. Serve with Fresh Tomato Salsa (p. 29) or Lime Cayenne Dip (p. 41).

◀ Makes 8 servings as 2-oz (60-g) fritters, ▶
or 12 servings as 1-oz (30-g) fritters

1 cup (250 mL) fresh corn (about 1 corn cob)

salt, to taste

ground black pepper, to taste

2 cups (500 mL) canola oil

1 medium onion, diced

1 celery stalk, diced

3 cups (750 mL) all-purpose flour

4 tsp baking powder

2 eggs, beaten

Preheat broiler or barbecue to medium.

In a large pot on high heat, blanch corn cob in salted boiling water for 5 minutes. Remove from water and submerge in ice-water bath (3 cups cold water to 1 cup ice). Season corn with salt, pepper, and olive oil. Place under broiler and roast 2–3 minutes per side, until golden brown. Cut kernels from cob and set aside.

In a bowl, combine corn, onions, and celery.

In a large bowl, combine flour, baking powder, eggs, and ¾ cup (185 mL) water until it forms a batter. Combine corn mixture and batter and let sit for 1 hour.

Preheat deep fryer to 350°F (180°C). Using a teaspoon, drop batter into hot oil and cook to a golden brown.

CORN BREAD

A perfect accompaniment to casseroles or stews, this moist, golden bread is best when enjoyed fresh out of the oven. The recipe can also be used to make muffins.

◄ Makes 1 loaf or 6 muffins ►

2½ cups (625 mL) all-purpose flour

2½ cups (625 mL) cornmeal

3½ tbsp baking powder

1 tsp salt

6 eggs, beaten

2½ cups (625 mL) milk

½ cup canola oil

Preheat oven to 400°F (200°C).

In a large bowl, combine flour, cornmeal, baking powder, and salt. Make a well in center of dry ingredients. Slowly stir in eggs, milk, and oil, just until smooth. Pour into an oiled 9 x 5-in (2-L) baking pan or standard muffin tin. Bake for 35 minutes, until golden brown.

BANNOCK (FRIED AND BAKED)

This bannock recipe was inspired by Mike House, the baker at the First Nations pavilion at Expo 86 in Vancouver. The recipe has evolved over time to reflect our healthier eating habits; I've removed the lard and reduced the salt content. I also use vegetable shortening when deep frying. You can use baked bannock instead of buns to make burgers for the Broiled Buffalo Patties (p. 90) or Gilled Pacific Salmon (p. 115).

1½ cups (375 mL) whole wheat flour

1½ cups (375 mL) all-purpose flour

3 heaping tbsp baking powder

3 tsp salt

3 tsp white sugar

4 cups (1 L) lukewarm water

FRIED BANNOCK
Makes 1 dozen bannock rounds

In a large bowl, combine all dry ingredients. Make a well in center and add water. Gently and quickly mix until ingredients just come together.

Preheat deep fryer to 350°F (180°C) or heat 2 tbsp oil in a large frying pan.

Place batter on floured surface and gently knead into soft dough, 3–4 minutes. Roll into a cylinder about 2½-in (6.35-cm) in diameter. Cut into 1-in (2.5-cm) thick rounds. Place on floured surface to rest for 10 minutes. In a deep fryer or frying pan, cook rounds about 7–8 minutes per side, until golden brown. Allow bannock rounds to cool, and slice in half like a burger bun.

BAKED BANNOCK
Makes 1 loaf

Note: Use slightly wetter dough to make baked bannock; increase water noted above as needed.

Preheat oven to 375°F (180°C). Follow recipe at left for preparing dough.

Place dough in an oiled and lightly floured loaf pan. Bake for 20 minutes. Remove from oven and brush top with soft butter, then bake for another 20 minutes. Remove bannock from pan and let rest on wire rack for at least 1 hour.

Cut bannock loaf into slices about 1-in (2.5-cm) thick.

PASTA
& PASTA
SAUCES

HOMEMADE SEMOLINA PASTA

This is a very good yet simple pasta dough. The semolina flour gives it a pleasingly firm texture and flavor. Serve topped with your favorite pasta sauce. (See pp. 146 and 147 for some delicious options.)

◄◄ **Makes enough for 8 servings** ►►

1 cup (250 mL) all-purpose flour

1 cup (250 mL) semolina flour

pinch of salt, for dough

3 large eggs

1 tbsp olive oil

4 tsp salt, for cooking noodles

On a large cutting board, sift together all-purpose and semolina flours with salt. Make a well in the center, break eggs into it, and add olive oil. Whisk with fork, gradually incorporating flour from sides of well. When mixture becomes too thick to mix with fork, knead with your hands for 8–12 minutes, until smooth. Wrap dough and let rest for 1 hour.

Cut dough into 4 segments. Roll through pasta machine to desired thickness. Cut into desired pasta shape, or leave in sheets for lasagna, ravioli, or cannelloni.

Bring a large pot of water and 4 tsp salt to a boil on high. Add pasta and cook for 8–12 minutes, depending on thickness. Strain well before topping or tossing with a sauce.

If this is your first attempt at making pasta, you may want to put wet and dry ingredients into separate bowls and then blend wet into dry.

HOMEMADE PASTA WITH ALL-PURPOSE FLOUR

This tender pasta dough is easy to knead. But beware, it cooks much faster than pasta made with semolina flour, quickly becoming mushy if not made a little thicker. It's great served with Fresh Tomato Sauce (p. 147).

◀■■ **Makes enough for 4 servings** ■■▶

1¾ cups (415 mL) all-purpose flour

3 eggs

1 tsp olive oil

1 tsp salt

On a large cutting board, add flour and make a well in the center. Break eggs into it, and stir in olive oil and salt. Whisk with a fork, gradually incorporating flour from sides of well. Add extra flour if dough is too moist, to keep it from sticking, or a little water, if too stiff. Once dough is shaped into a firm and manageable ball, knead with your hands for 8–12 minutes, until smooth. Wrap dough and let rest for 1 hour. Cut dough into 4 segments. Roll through pasta machine to desired thickness. Cut into desired pasta shape, or leave in sheets for lasagna, ravioli, or cannelloni.

Bring a large pot of water and 4 tsp salt to a boil on high. Add pasta and cook for 8–12 minutes, depending on thickness. Strain well before topping or tossing with a sauce.

DANDELION GREENS FETTUCCINI

Here is a neat take on making green pasta. Serve as a side with chicken and seafood or as a main topped with Wild Game Bolognese Sauce (p. 146).

◄ Makes enough for 4–6 servings ►

2 cups (500 mL) chopped raw dandelion greens

2 eggs

½ tsp salt

1½ cup (375 mL) all-purpose flour

In a blender, process greens with eggs until smooth. Pour into a bowl. Add salt and flour while stirring with a spoon to blend. Dough should be firm; if it isn't, add more flour. Turn onto floured surface and knead until smooth, about 5 minutes. Using a pasta machine, follow directions to make fettuccini.

To make fettuccini without a pasta machine, roll out dough with rolling pin to ⅛–¼-in (3–6-mm) thickness. Allow to dry for 1 hour. Cut into strips ¼ in (6 mm) wide. Drop into boiling, salted water for 1–2 minutes.

WILD GAME BOLOGNESE SAUCE

This is a great-tasting, chunky sauce, bursting with fresh flavors. Serve it over spaghetti, rigatoni, or tagliatelle noodles and sprinkle with freshly grated Parmesan cheese.

◀ Makes 4 cups (1 L) ▶

3 tbsp extra-virgin olive oil

½ lb (250 g) ground buffalo

½ lb (250 g) ground venison (or ground beef)

½ lb (250 g) ground wild boar (or ground pork)

½ cup (125 mL) finely chopped onions

1 tbsp minced garlic

1 cup (250 mL) red wine

1 28-oz (796-mL) can whole tomatoes, chopped, strained, liquid reserved

1 bay leaf

1 tbsp chopped fresh oregano

1 tbsp chopped fresh basil

sea salt, to taste

ground black pepper, to taste

In a heavy saucepan, heat olive oil on medium-high. Brown buffalo, venison, and wild boar meat. Add onions and cook for 2 minutes, until tender. Add garlic and cook until golden, about 2 minutes. Add red wine and simmer until lightly reduced, about 5 minutes. Add both tomatoes and reserved liquid to onion mixture and bring to a boil. Reduce heat to low and add bay leaf, oregano, and basil. Let simmer, uncovered, until sauce thickens, about 45 minutes. Adjust consistency, if desired, with about ¼ cup (60 mL) cold water. Season to taste. Discard bay leaf before serving.

FRESH TOMATO SAUCE

In the SuperChefs program, I teach young people basic culinary skills. We use this classic sauce over Homemade Pasta (p. 142 or 143)—but it's a perfect complement to any pasta dish.

Makes 4 cups (1 L)

3 tbsp olive oil

½ cup (125 mL) finely chopped onion

1 tbsp minced garlic

1 28-oz (796-mL) can whole tomatoes

1 bay leaf

1 tbsp chopped fresh oregano

1 tbsp chopped fresh basil

sea salt, to taste

ground black pepper, to taste

In a heavy saucepan on medium-high, heat oil. Add onions and cook for 2 minutes until tender and translucent. Add garlic and cook until golden brown, about 2 minutes. Strain tomatoes and reserve liquid in a bowl. Chop tomatoes, add to pan, and bring to a boil, then reduce to a simmer. Add bay leaf. Cook until sauce thickens, about 45 minutes. Adjust consistency if needed with reserved tomato juice. Add fresh herbs, salt, and pepper to taste. Discard bay leaf before serving.

WEST COAST SEAFOOD PASTA

This dish is all about celebrating the flavors of the fresh seafood we enjoy here on the West Coast.

◀ **Makes 4–6 servings** ▶

1 lb (500 g) dry rotini

¼ cup (60 mL) butter

2 medium onions, diced

4 garlic cloves, minced

16 medium Manila clams

1 cup (250 mL) white wine, for clams

8 whole Pacific prawns, cleaned and deveined

6 large scallops

4 oz (115 g) wild Pacific salmon, cubed

4 oz (115 g) fresh Pacific halibut, cubed

½ cup (125 mL) white wine, for seafood

2 tbsp dill pesto (p.26)

2 cups (500 mL) fish velouté (p. 23)

salt, to taste

ground black pepper, to taste

1½ tsp red chili flakes

In a large pot of boiling, salted water on high heat, cook rotini for 8 minutes, until al dente. Strain and set aside to cool.

In a large saucepan on medium heat, melt butter. Sauté onions and garlic for 5–7 minutes, until translucent. Add clams and 1 cup white wine. Cover and allow to steam for 3–4 minutes, or until clams open. Add prawns, scallops, salmon, and halibut, ½ cup white wine, and dill pesto. Let simmer for 2 minutes. Add fish velouté and continue to simmer for 2 more minutes. Add cooked rotini and season with salt and pepper. Continue to cook for 3–4 minutes. Garnish with sprinkle of red chili flakes.

SMOKED SALMON LINGUINE

I learned how to make this rich and creamy dish at the Avenue Grill, a landmark restaurant in Vancouver's Kerrisdale neighborhood where I started my culinary apprenticeship in 1986. It's still on the menu!

Makes 4 servings

½ lb (250 g) fresh linguine

¼ cup (60 mL) cream cheese

2 tbsp white wine

3 sprigs fresh dill, chopped, or 1 tsp dried dill

1½ cups (375 mL) fish velouté (p. 23)

2 garlic cloves, minced

½ cup (125 mL) 35% cream

1½ lb (750 g) smoked salmon

¼ cup (60 mL) freshly grated Parmesan cheese

salt, to taste

ground black pepper, to taste

4 green onions, thinly sliced, for garnish

In a large pot of boiling, salted water, cook linguine until al dente, about 2–3 minutes for fresh pasta; follow package directions if using dried. Strain and set aside to cool.

In a medium saucepan on medium heat, combine cream cheese, wine, dill, fish velouté, and garlic. Simmer until reduced by half. Stir in cream, smoked salmon, and Parmesan cheese and continue to simmer. Add linguine and simmer for 2–3 minutes. Season with salt and pepper. Garnish with green onions.

BUTTERNUT SQUASH & PEAR RAVIOLI

Squash and pears make a velvety golden and slightly sweet filling for tender homemade ravioli. Top with your favorite pesto (pp. 25–28) or sauce of your choice.

◀ **Makes 6 servings** ▶

1 butternut squash

4 tbsp olive oil

salt, to taste

ground white pepper, to taste

¼ cup (60 mL) shredded Parmesan cheese

¼ tsp chili powder

1 large pear, peeled, cored, and diced

salt, to taste

ground white pepper, to taste

1 lb (500g) homemade pasta dough (p.143)

Preheat oven to 350°F (180°C).

Cut squash in half lengthwise and remove seeds. Rub with oil and season with salt and pepper. Bake for 45 minutes. Let cool and scrape out flesh. In a large, unoiled frying pan on medium heat, cook squash for 10 minutes. Remove and place in bowl. Add Parmesan cheese, chili powder, and pear. Season with salt and pepper and set aside.

Roll pasta dough out to 1/16-in (1.5-cm) thick sheets. Place 1-tsp scoops of mixture on dough, 1 in (2.5 cm) apart. Lightly brush water around each scoop of mixture, then place a sheet of fresh pasta on top. Press top piece of dough around scoops to get rid of air pockets and seal edges well. Cut into ravioli squares using a sharp knife or pizza cutter or, using a glass, cut out circles around each mound.

In a large pot of boiling salted water, cook ravioli for 4–5 minutes, until tender.

VENISON FETTUCCINI

This recipe combines two of my favorite foods: pasta and venison. The soy sauce marinade will make the venison tender and delicious.

Makes 4 servings

1 lb (500 g) boneless venison (or beef or chicken breasts), sliced into ¾-in (2-cm) strips

2 tbsp soy sauce, for marinade

2 garlic cloves, minced, for marinade

2 tsp minced ginger, for marinade

1 tbsp oil

1 each red and yellow bell peppers, seeded and sliced into strips

1 small zucchini, sliced diagonally

1 carrot, sliced diagonally

1 cup (250 mL) fiddleheads

2 tbsp light soy sauce

2 tbsp red wine

½ cup (125 mL) demi-glace (p. 20)

1 lb (500 g) cooked fettuccini noodles

¼ cup (60 mL) toasted cashews (optional), for garnish

In a large glass dish, marinate venison strips in soy sauce, garlic, and ginger for 2–4 hours.

In a large frying pan on high, heat oil to smoking point, and quickly sauté venison until browned. Remove from pan. Reduce heat to medium. Add vegetables and sauté for 2 minutes. Pour in light soy sauce, wine, and demi-glace, and bring to a simmer for 3–4 minutes. Add fettuccini, toss, and serve topped with cashews.

MOOSE CANNELLONI

The spinach, cheese, and prosciutto (aged, dry-cured Italian ham) complement the moose meat to make this a tasty and hearty dish.

◀━━━ Makes 8 rolls, 4 servings ━━━▶

3 tbsp extra-virgin olive oil

2 lb (1 kg) ground moose meat (or venison, beef, or veal)

1 small onion, chopped

2 garlic cloves, finely chopped

10 oz (300 g) baby spinach

1¾ cups (415 mL) ricotta cheese (12 oz fresh, or 15 oz supermarket-style)

1 large egg, lightly beaten

½ cup (125 mL) chopped fresh flat-leaf parsley

3 oz (90 g) thinly sliced prosciutto (optional)

¼ tsp salt

¼ tsp ground black pepper

⅓ cup (80 mL) finely grated Parmesan or Romano cheese, for filling

8 6 x 4-in fresh pasta rectangles (see homemade pasta, p. 143)

⅔ cup (160 mL) fresh tomato sauce (p. 147), for filling

3⅓ cups (820 mL) fresh tomato sauce (p. 147), for topping

¼ cup (60 mL) finely grated Parmesan or Romano cheese, for topping

Preheat oven to 425°F (220°C).

In a 5–6 quart (L) heavy pot, heat oil on medium-high, until hot but not smoking. Sauté moose meat, onions, and garlic, stirring occasionally, until lightly browned, about 15 minutes. Add spinach and sauté, stirring until wilted, about 3 minutes. Remove from heat and let cool completely.

In a large bowl, combine ricotta, egg, parsley, prosciutto, salt, pepper, and ⅓ cup Parmesan cheese. Stir into meat mixture. Set aside.

In a large pot of boiling salted water, cook pasta rectangles 2 pieces at a time. Stir if necessary to keep from sticking and cook until just tender, about 2 minutes. Using a slotted spoon, gently transfer pasta to a large bowl of cold water to stop cooking. Remove from bowl, shake off water, and lay flat on dry kitchen towels (not terrycloth).

Pat pasta dry with paper towels. Pour ⅔ cup tomato sauce into lightly oiled large casserole dish. Place ⅓ cup ricotta filling in a line along one short side of one pasta rectangle, then roll up to enclose filling. Transfer, seam side down, to baking dish. Make 7 more cannelloni in same manner, arranging snugly in 1 layer. Pour ½ cup remaining tomato sauce over cannelloni, and sprinkle with ¼ cup grated Parmesan cheese.

Cover baking dish with foil and bake, on middle rack of oven, until sauce is bubbling, about 20 minutes. Turn on broiler. Remove foil and move cannelloni to rack about 5 in (12 cm) from heat. Broil until lightly browned, 2–4 minutes. Let stand 5 minutes before serving.

Instead of homemade pasta, you can use store-bought, oven-ready canneloni shells. Stuff shells with filling before baking.

DESSERTS

BANNOCK BREAD PUDDING WITH CRÈME ANGLAISE & CARAMEL SAUCE

This is inspired by a comfort-food recipe that Grandma used to make. It's so sinfully delicious, especially topped with the Crème Anglaise and Caramel Sauce, you may not be able to eat another dessert for a year!

◄ Makes 6–8 servings ►

1 tbsp butter, for pan

¼ cup (60 mL) white sugar

2 cups (500 mL) whole milk

4 eggs, separated

1 cup (250 mL) loosely packed brown sugar

1 tsp ground cinnamon

1 tsp vanilla extract

5½ cups (1.4 L) cubed baked bannock (p. 138)

½ cup (125 mL) raisins

Preheat oven to 350°F (190°C).

Butter an 8 x 8-in (2-L) soufflé mold and sprinkle with white sugar. In a large bowl, mix milk, egg yolks, brown sugar, cinnamon, and vanilla. Stir in bannock and raisins. Let mixture soak for 10 minutes.

In another bowl, use an electric beater to whip egg whites until firm peaks form. Using a spatula, slowly fold meringue into bread mixture. Bake for 1 hour, until center is firm and moist.

Serve each portion with a dollop of crème anglaise and caramel sauce.

CRÈME ANGLAISE
Makes about 1 cup (250 mL)

½ cup (125 mL) milk
½ cup (125 mL) whipping cream
½ tsp vanilla extract
1 tbsp sugar, for hot cream mixture
3 egg yolks
1 tbsp sugar, for eggs

In a small saucepan on medium heat, bring milk, cream, vanilla extract, and 1 tbsp sugar to a slow simmer.

In a medium bowl, whisk egg yolks and remaining sugar to combine well. Slowly fold in hot cream mixture 1 tbsp at a time. Pour back into saucepan and return to medium heat until it starts to thicken, around 2–3 minutes.

CARAMEL SAUCE
Makes about 4 cups (1 l)

2 cups (500 mL) white sugar
2 tbsp lemon juice
1 tbsp water
4 cups (1 L) 35% whipping cream

In a medium saucepan on medium heat, melt sugar, lemon juice, and water. Cook mixture until sugar has caramelized or browned. Reduce heat to low and slowly whisk in cream until smooth.

Caution: liquid will be very hot, and if cream is added too quickly, will boil over.

APPLE BERRY CRISP

Serve this on a cold winter's night hot out of the oven, topped with ice cream.

◀━━ ▮ **Makes 6 servings** ▮ ━━▶

4 cups (1 L) sliced apples

1 cup (250 mL) berries (blueberries, strawberries, etc., or mixture)

½ cup (125 mL) apple juice

⅔ cup (160 mL) packed brown sugar

¼ cup (60 mL) flour

¾ cup (185 mL) rolled oats

1½ tsp ground cinnamon

⅓ cup butter, room temperature

Preheat oven to 375°F (190°C).

Lightly oil an 8 x 8 in (2 L) pan. Place apples and berries in pan. In a medium bowl, mix remaining ingredients and sprinkle over fruit mixture. Bake for 30 minutes, until apples are tender and top is browned.

WILD BERRY COBBLER

This is a recipe our mother used to make during huckleberry season. It goes great with ice cream.

◀ **Makes 12–16 servings** ▶

1 gallon (4 L) fresh huckleberries, raspberries, blueberries, or frozen mixed berries

2 cups (500 mL) sugar

¼ cup (60 mL) tapioca

2½ cups (625 mL) water

1½ tsp lemon zest

¼ cup (60 mL) unsalted butter

In a large bowl combine all ingredients, tossing until berries are coated.

STREUSEL TOPPING

1 cup (250 mL) all-purpose flour

1½ tsp ground cinnamon

1 tsp salt

1 cup (250 mL) brown sugar

3 cups (750 mL) sugar

2½ cups (625 mL) butter

Preheat oven to 350°F (180°C).

Lightly butter an 8 x 12 in (20 x 30 cm) baking dish. Pour in berry mixture.

For the streusel:
In a bowl, combine ingredients. Cut in butter until mixture is coarse and crumbly.

Top berries with streusel mixture. Bake for about 40–50 minutes, until berry mixture bubbles and top is lightly browned.

MAPLE QUENELLES WITH FRESH MANGO PURÉE & CHOCOLATE SAUCE

*Quenelle is a French term that comes from the German **Knidel**, which means dumpling. But these are no ordinary dumplings—they're light and fine in texture, and sweet in taste. Freshly puréed mangos and rich chocolate sauce are the perfect accompaniments. For a lighter dessert, serve with seasonal berries.*

◄ Makes 4 servings (12 quenelles) ►

3 egg yolks

⅓ cup (80 mL) icing sugar

3 sheets gelatin, soaked and melted

1⅓ cups (330 mL) 35% whipping cream

½ cup (125 mL) maple syrup

1 tbsp brandy

2 ripe mangos

½ cup (125 mL) chocolate sauce (below)

CHOCOLATE SAUCE
Makes about ½ cup (125 ml)

½ cup (125 mL) 35% cream

¼ cup (60 mL) semi-sweet chocolate chips

½ tsp vanilla extract

½ tsp white sugar (optional)

In a medium stainless steel bowl over a pot of boiling water, whisk cream, chocolate chips, vanilla, and sugar until chocolate is melted. Place in refrigerator to chill for at least 4 hours before serving.

In a double boiler or a medium stainless steel bowl over a pot of boiling water, beat egg yolks and sugar until fully incorporated, pale yellow, and creamy, about 3 minutes. Remove from heat and stir in melted gelatin until well combined.

In a separate medium bowl, whip cream until soft peaks form. Fold cream into yolk mixture, and add maple syrup and brandy. Use 2 dessert spoons to make egg-shaped quenelles: scoop a dessert spoon of mixture, then pass from one spoon to the other until formed. Carefully place quenelles onto pan lined with wax paper. Place in refrigerator to chill.

Peel mangos, and cut flesh away from pits. In a food processor, purée mangos until smooth. To serve, arrange 3 quenelles on a plate. Decorate plates with mango purée and chocolate sauce.

WHIPPED SOOPOLLALIE BERRIES WITH SABAYON

Also known as soapberries, soopollalie berries are native to British Columbia and will foam like soap when whipped. Sweet Madeira wine complements the bitterness of the berries perfectly. Serve with a sabayon, a light, custard-like dessert (below).

Makes 4 servings

3 tbsp fresh soopollalie berries

3 tbsp cold water

¼ cup (60 mL) Madeira wine

¼–½ cup (60–125 mL) sugar

SABAYON

8 egg yolks

⅔ cup (160 mL) sugar

¾ cup (185 mL) Madeira wine

2 tbsp lemon juice

In a small stainless steel bowl, crush berries, making sure to extract juice. Stir in cold water and Madeira. With a hand blender, whisk berries rapidly while slowly adding sugar until stiff peaks are formed (do not add sugar too fast or it will bind).

For the sabayon:
In a stainless steel bowl over a pot of simmering hot water, whisk egg yolks and sugar until pale and creamy. When mixture is foamy, stir in Madeira 1 tbsp at a time while continuing to whisk. Stir in lemon juice and continue to whisk. Keep whisking until sauce thickens, about 10 minutes.

SASKATOON PIE

This was my father's favorite pie. Cree in origin, the city of Saskatoon, Saskatchewan was named for the berry.

◀━━━━ **Makes 1 pie** ▶━━━

¾ cup (185 mL) granulated sugar

3 tbsp flour

4 cups (1 L) Saskatoon berries (a.k.a. serviceberries)

¼ cup (60 mL) water

2 tbsp lemon juice

¼ cup (60 mL) butter

pastry for two-crust pie

Preheat oven to 425°F (220°C).

In a small bowl, combine sugar and flour. In a saucepan on medium-high heat, simmer berries in water for 10 minutes. Add lemon juice, and stir into sugar-flour mixture. Pour into pastry-lined pie plate; dot with butter. Cover with top crust. Seal and flute edges. Bake for 15 minutes. Reduce heat to 350°F (180°C) and bake 35–45 minutes longer, until golden brown.

SWEET POTATO PIE

This is a popular item on our catering menus. People really love this pie!
Top it with whipped cream and chopped toasted hazelnuts.

◀◀ **Makes 1 pie** ▶▶

2 eggs

1½ cups (375 mL) baked sweet potatoes, mashed

1 cup (250 mL) brown sugar

1 tsp ground cinnamon

½ tsp ground nutmeg

¼ tsp ground ginger

¼ tsp salt

¾ cup (185 mL) evaporated milk

pie shell, baked until golden

Preheat oven to 350°F (180°C).

In a medium bowl, lightly beat eggs. Stir in sweet potatoes, sugar, cinnamon, nutmeg, ginger, and salt. Stir in milk until well combined. Pour filling into baked pie shell, and bake for 45 minutes, until toothpick inserted into center of pie comes out clean.

BREAKFASTS

BREAKFAST PARFAIT

We use this recipe in the SuperChefs program to promote healthy breakfast-eating habits among kids. It's a delicious way to start the day—for kids or grownups.

Makes 4 servings

4 cups (1 L) chopped mixed berries (strawberries, blueberries, blackberries, raspberries, etc.)

1 tbsp chopped fresh mint

1 tbsp honey

4 cups (1 L) vanilla yogurt

2 cups (500 mL) granola

In a medium bowl, combine fresh berries, mint, and honey. Set aside. In a large glass bowl, layer 1 cup (250 mL) yogurt, ½ cup (125 mL) granola, and 1 cup (250 mL) berry mixture. Repeat layers until all ingredients are used.

SASKATOON BERRY-STUFFED FRENCH TOAST

I created this recipe for special weekend cooking sessions with my own kids when they were little. They loved the French toast, and so did we.

Makes 4 servings

8 thick slices bread (French or Italian work well, especially when day-old)

8 oz (230 g) cream cheese, softened

½ cup (125 mL) Saskatoon or blueberry jam

5 eggs

¼ cup (60 mL) milk

1½ tsp vanilla extract

1 tbsp butter (or margarine)

Spread 4 slices of bread with cream cheese on one side. Spread one side of remaining 4 slices with jam. Press together, plain sides out, to form 4 sandwiches.

In a medium shallow bowl, beat eggs, milk, and vanilla extract.

In a large, heavy frying pan on medium-high heat, melt butter. Dip sandwiches into egg mixture to coat. Place in skillet and cook until golden-brown, then flip and repeat.

WILD HUCKLEBERRY PANCAKES WITH HUCKLEBERRY SAUCE

The touch of cumin in this recipe, while optional, adds an earthy flavor to the pancakes that perfectly complements the sweet wild huckleberries. It's a great way to begin the weekend, and is even better if you make this with your kids, who will love it! Our kids certainly did.

◀ **Makes 14 4-in (10-cm) pancakes** ▶

1½ cups (375 mL) sifted all-purpose flour

1 tsp salt

2 tbsp sugar

2 tsp baking powder

1 egg

3 tbsp melted butter

1¼ cups (310 mL) milk

2 cups (500 mL) wild huckleberries (or blueberries)

1 tsp cumin (optional)

HUCKLEBERRY SAUCE

4 cups (1 L) fresh huckleberries

½ cup (125 mL) sugar (or honey)

2 tbsp lemon juice

1 tsp lemon zest

1 tsp chopped fresh mint leaves

1 tsp vanilla extract

Over a large pitcher, resift flour with salt, sugar, and baking powder.

In a small bowl, beat egg. Mix in butter and milk. Stir in huckleberries and cumin. Stir into flour mixture. Pour batter onto a hot lightly oiled griddle or frying pan. Cook about 2–3 minutes, turning only once. Cook other side for 2–3 minutes. Top with huckleberry sauce.

For the sauce:
In a food processor, pulse all ingredients together briefly so mixture remains chunky. Serve chilled.

PEACH-STUFFED CHEESE BLINTZES WITH WILD BERRY SAUCE

Blintzes (a.k.a. blinis) are Russian egg-batter pancakes that can be stuffed with either sweet or savory fillings. Here, they make a special breakfast or brunch, served with a wild berry sauce.

◀ Makes 16–18 blintzes ▶

BLINTZES

⅞ cup (210 mL) all-purpose flour

pinch salt

3 eggs

1–1½ cups (250 mL–375 mL) milk

2 tbsp melted butter

In a large bowl, sift together flour and salt. In a small bowl, lightly beat eggs. Using a wooden spoon, make a well in center of flour and pour in eggs. Slowly pour ¾ cup (185 mL) milk and butter into well, gradually working into flour with spoon. When fully incorporated, beat mixture vigorously with either a wooden spoon, whisk, or hand or electric mixer, until it becomes smooth (no lumps). Allow mixture to stand for 3–5 minutes. Add enough of remaining milk, beating continuously, to make a thin batter with the consistency of light cream.

In an 8–10 in (20–25 cm) iron non-stick pan on medium heat, pour ½ cup (125 mL) batter, and tilt pan in all directions to coat bottom of pan. Cook until batter is golden brown, about 3–4 minutes. Flip with rubber spatula and cook for another 3–4 minutes. Repeat until all batter is used up.

FILLING

2 cups (500 mL) cottage cheese

¼ cup (60 mL) powdered sugar

¼ tsp vanilla extract

1 tsp ground cinnamon

¼ tsp ground allspice

1 cup (250 mL) cubed, canned peaches

In a large bowl, mix all ingredients together. Chill in refrigerator until needed.

WILD BERRY SAUCE

1 tbsp cornstarch

4 cups (1 L) wild huckleberries or your favorite berries

1 tsp vanilla extract

½ cup (125 mL) sugar (or honey)

1 tbsp orange zest

Preheat oven to 350°F (180°C).

In a medium bowl, thoroughly combine cornstarch with ½ cup (125 mL) cold water.

In a small saucepan on high heat, bring berries, 1 cup (250 mL) water, vanilla extract, sugar, and orange zest to a boil. Reduce heat to low and simmer for 10 minutes. Remove from heat and set aside.

To assemble, add 2 tsp of filling to each blintz and roll up. Place rolled blintzes into an 8-in (20 cm) baking dish, and pour sauce over blintzes. Bake for 10–12 minutes.

VENISON SAUSAGE OMELETTE

This classic omelette features venison sausage, but I've included options so you can create any kind of omelette you like, or make several kinds to suit either vegetarians or meat eaters. This is a great opportunity for you to get creative!

◀ **Makes 1 serving** ▶

2 eggs

1 tbsp milk or water

salt, to taste

ground black pepper, to taste

1 tsp butter

¼–⅓ cup (60–80 mL) crumbled and browned
   venison sausage

¼–⅓ cup (60–80 mL) freshly grated aged cheddar,
   Swiss, or Monterey Jack cheese

FILLING OPTIONS

¼–⅓ cup (60–80 mL) chopped and sautéed mixed
   vegetables (onions, bell peppers, asparagus,
   green beans, etc.)

¼–⅓ cup (60–80 mL) smoked salmon

To any or all of the above, add:

1 tbsp minced fresh or 1 tsp dried herbs of your choice
   (e.g., basil, rosemary, oregano, parsley)

In a mixing bowl, beat eggs with a fork. Add milk or water, salt, and pepper. Set aside. In a 6–8 in (15–20 cm) omelette pan on high heat, melt butter, coating bottom of pan evenly. As soon as butter stops sizzling and bubbling, but before it turns brown, add eggs. Tilt pan to spread eggs evenly. Cook until eggs have slightly firmed. Coax edges to center of pan with a spatula, and then tilt pan to allow liquid to coat and firm up again at edges of pan. Continue to cook for 1 minute, until eggs are set. While middle is still a little runny, add venison to center, and top with cheese. Tilt pan to one side, and use spatula to fold omelette in half.

FRITTATA WITH FETTUCCINI

This is a very filling and delicious breakfast.

◀ **Makes 6 servings** ▶

1 tsp salt

12-oz (355-mL) dry fettuccini

2 tbsp extra-virgin olive oil

2 tbsp butter

1 cup (250 mL) heavy cream

1 cup (250 mL) freshly grated Parmesan cheese

¼–½ tsp grated or ground nutmeg

salt, to taste

ground black pepper, to taste

¼ cup (60 mL) chopped flat-leaf parsley

12 extra-large eggs, beaten

Preheat oven to 425°F (220°C).

Bring a large pot of water to a boil and add 1 tsp salt. Add fettuccini and cook for 6 minutes, until al dente. (Pasta will continue to cook in frittata.) Strain and set aside.

In a large, non-stick frying pan on medium-high heat, melt oil and butter. Add cream and simmer until reduced by half. Stir in cheese, nutmeg, salt, and pepper. Add fettuccini and stir to combine well. Add parsley and beaten eggs to pan, and stir gently to combine. Cook until eggs have set and become firm. Transfer pan to hot oven and bake for 10 minutes, until golden. Cut into wedges and serve hot or cold.

BANNOCK BENNIES WITH SMOKED SALMON

A classic dish—Eggs Benedict—with bannock and smoked salmon standing in for crumpets and ham.
If you're health-conscious, go easy on the hollandaise!

◀ **Makes 4 servings** ▶

8 eggs, poached (opposite)

4 rounds deep-fried bannock, split lengthwise (p.138)

4 tbsp cream cheese (or 3 tbsp goat cheese and
   1 tbsp plain yogurt—my favorite)

1 cup (250 mL) arugula

4 slices smoked salmon (approximately 3–4 oz,
   or 100 g), cut in half (8 pieces total)

1 cup (250 mL) hollandaise sauce (opposite)

salt, to taste

ground black pepper, to taste

While eggs are poaching, toast bannock halves under broiler or in a toaster. Spread cream cheese on one side of toasted bannock. Assemble bennies by placing arugula on bannock, then smoked salmon. Top with 2 poached eggs and finish with a dollop of hollandaise sauce. Season with salt and pepper.

PERFECTLY POACHED EGGS
4 cups (1 L) water
2 tsp white vinegar
8 eggs

For best results, let eggs sit at room temperature for at least an hour before poaching. In a small saucepan, bring water and vinegar to a boil; reduce to slow simmer. Crack eggs into small ramekin or bowl before adding to water. Stir water, then add eggs. Poach for 4 minutes. Remove and strain.

HOLLANDAISE SAUCE
Makes 2 cups (500 ml)

15 crushed peppercorns
4 parsley stalks
2 tsp finely chopped shallots
2 tsp malt vinegar
2 tsp white wine vinegar
6 egg yolks
1 lb (500 g) clarified butter
fresh lemon juice, to taste
Tabasco sauce, to taste

In a small saucepan on medium heat, add peppercorns, parsley, shallots, and malt and wine vinegar. Cook until reduced by half. Strain into a clean bowl.

In a stainless steel bowl over a pot of simmering water, add egg yolks and vinegar mixture. With a whisk, beat egg yolks until slightly thickened. Remove bowl from heat often to prevent overcooking. When mixture has increased in volume, slowly add clarified butter, whisking constantly as sauce thickens. Do not let it get too thick. Whisk in lemon juice and Tabasco. Add a little hot water if too thick. Keep sauce warm until ready to be served (will keep for no longer than 2 hours).

SMOKED TROUT HASH WITH GRILLED SALMON & POACHED EGGS

We used to go fishing for trout and salmon with my parents on our traditional territories. The Hollandaise sauce is optional but sure adds to the dish.

◀ **Makes 4 servings** ▶

2 tbsp olive oil

4 Yukon gold potatoes, diced

1 large red onion, diced

1 fillet Hot Smoked Trout, slivered (p. 39)

4 Grilled Pacific Salmon with Fresh Herbs (p. 115) (or steak)

8 eggs, poached (p. 179)

1 cup (250 mL) hollandaise sauce (optional) (p. 179)

In a large frying pan on medium-high, heat oil and sauté potatoes until lightly browned.

Add onions and sauté for 7–10 minutes more, until browned. Stir in smoked trout and sauté for another 3 minutes.

On serving plate, top hash with 1 grilled salmon fillet and 2 poached eggs. Top with hollandaise sauce, if desired, and serve hot.

VENISON HASH

After my father or uncles would come back from hunting trips, we would enjoy this hash on crisp fall mornings. It was, and still is, a treat. Serve with warm baked bannock (p.138).

Makes 4 servings

¼ cup (60 mL) canola oil

1 lb (500 g) venison (or beef), sliced into ¼-in (6-mm) strips

3 cloves roasted garlic

¼ cup (60 mL) venison stock (p.18)

6 Yukon gold potatoes, diced and cooked (best if cooked the night before)

1 large onion, diced

salt, to taste

ground black pepper, to taste

1 tsp chopped fresh rosemary, for garnish

8 eggs, poached (p. 179)

In a large cast-iron frying pan on high, heat oil to smoking point. Reduce heat to medium. Add venison and stir-fry with garlic until venison is browned. Remove and set aside. Deglaze pan with stock, and add potatoes and onions. Cook until stock has almost evaporated. Season with salt and pepper, and garnish with rosemary. On plates, top each serving of hash with 2 poached eggs.

ACKNOWLEDGMENTS

I would like to extend my sincerest thanks to all the chefs who taught me the wonderful trade of cooking, and inspired me to become the professional chef I am today. They have shared their knowledge with me, and are the reason for all of the recipes in this book.

I would like to thank all of the chefs and instructors at the Vancouver Vocational Institute, now Vancouver Community College, as well as the chefs and instructors at the old Pacific Vocational Institute, part of the British Columbia Institute of Technology, for introducing me to, and teaching me, the basics of professional cooking.

Thanks to the chefs who took me in for my apprentice-ship, including my mentor Dorothy Lillace, who gave me a chance to prove myself as an apprentice for a year and a half at the Avenue Grill in Kerrisdale, South Vancouver. Chef Wolfgang at the Four Seasons Hotel in Vancouver and Chef Hubertus at Isadora's on Granville Island in Vancouver were also invaluable to my education for sharing their enthusiasm, patience, and vast culinary knowledge.

Thank you to all the instructors and industry chefs that were, and still are, involved in developing and supporting initiatives for training young Aboriginal people in the trade of cooking, including those who helped me train in Toronto and Montreal prior to the 1992 World Culinary Olympics.

I would like to thank my parents, Rita George (Gihl-Lakh-Khan) and the late Andrew George Sr (Tsabassa), for their traditional teachings, as well as for their foresight in encouraging my siblings and me toward a western education. Their unending support—and care packages containing traditional foods like smoked salmon, moose, and berries—we now pass on to our own children as they move forward in life.

Thank you to the Wet'suwet'en Hereditary Chiefs, who groomed me and taught me the importance of being proud of who you are and where you come from. Their support led me to get a hereditary wing chief name in 1997, and encouraged me to relay their teachings to future generations.

Finally, I would like to thank Robert Gairns for his dedication in helping me write the first book, *Feast!: Canadian Native Cuisine for All Seasons,* and the re-release, *A Feast for all Seasons: Traditional Native Peoples' Cuisine*. I would also like to thank him for inspiring me to write about Aboriginal cuisine in the first place. Without him, none of these books would exist.

Sincerely,
Andrew George Jr.

INDEX